50 American Ramen Recipes for Home

By: Kelly Johnson

Table of Contents

- Classic Tonkotsu Ramen
- Spicy Miso Ramen
- Shoyu Ramen
- Vegetarian Ramen
- Chicken Ramen
- Beef Ramen
- Seafood Ramen
- Kimchi Ramen
- Vegan Miso Ramen
- Pork Belly Ramen
- Garlic Sesame Ramen
- Curry Ramen
- Creamy Chicken Ramen
- Thai Coconut Ramen
- Ramen Carbonara
- Ramen with Poached Egg
- Ramen with Grilled Tofu
- Ramen Stir-Fry
- Ramen Salad
- Ramen Burger
- Ramen Pizza
- Ramen Burrito
- Ramen Tacos
- Ramen Casserole
- Ramen Sliders
- Ramen Sushi Rolls
- Ramen Macaroni and Cheese
- Ramen Risotto
- Ramen Stuffed Peppers
- Ramen Stew
- Ramen Gyoza
- Ramen Spring Rolls
- Ramen Quiche
- Ramen Frittata
- Ramen Omelette

- Ramen Breakfast Bowl
- Ramen Hash Browns
- Ramen Pancakes
- Ramen Donuts
- Ramen Ice Cream
- Ramen Pudding
- Ramen Cheesecake
- Ramen Cookies
- Ramen Granola Bars
- Ramen Smoothie
- Ramen Cocktail
- Ramen Infused Water
- Ramen Tea
- Ramen Lemonade
- Ramen Energy Drink

Classic Tonkotsu Ramen

Broth:

Ingredients:

- 2-3 pounds pork bones (neck bones, trotters, or hocks)
- 1 onion, halved
- 1 knob ginger, sliced
- 2 cloves garlic, smashed
- 1 leek, chopped
- 2 carrots, chopped
- 1/2 cup sake (optional)
- Water

Instructions:

1. **Prepare the bones:** If using fresh pork bones, blanch them in boiling water for 10 minutes to remove impurities.
2. **Simmer the broth:** In a large pot, combine pork bones, onion, ginger, garlic, leek, carrots, and sake (if using). Add enough water to cover everything.
3. **Bring to a boil:** Skim off any scum that rises to the surface. Reduce heat to low and simmer gently for at least 8 hours, ideally 12-15 hours, adding water as needed to keep ingredients submerged.
4. **Strain the broth:** Once the broth has a creamy white color and a rich pork flavor, strain it through a fine mesh sieve or cheesecloth. Discard solids.
5. **Season the broth:** Season with salt and optionally a bit of soy sauce or miso paste to taste. Keep warm until ready to serve.

Noodles:

Ingredients:

- Fresh ramen noodles (or dried if fresh are unavailable)
- Water for boiling

Instructions:

1. **Cook the noodles:** Boil water in a separate pot and cook the ramen noodles according to package instructions (usually about 1-2 minutes for fresh noodles).
2. **Drain and rinse:** Drain the noodles and rinse under cold water to stop the cooking process. This helps maintain a firm texture.

Toppings:

- Chashu pork (braised pork belly slices)

- Soft-boiled eggs (seasoned with soy sauce and mirin)
- Bamboo shoots (menma)
- Nori (seaweed sheets)
- Green onions, finely chopped
- Corn kernels (optional)

Assembly:

1. **Prepare bowls:** Divide cooked noodles among serving bowls.
2. **Add toppings:** Arrange chashu pork slices, soft-boiled egg halves, bamboo shoots, nori, green onions, and corn over the noodles.
3. **Pour broth:** Ladle hot Tonkotsu broth over the noodles and toppings.
4. **Serve immediately:** Enjoy your homemade Classic Tonkotsu Ramen piping hot!

This recipe provides a traditional base, but feel free to adjust seasoning and toppings to suit your preferences. Enjoy your homemade ramen experience!

Spicy Miso Ramen

Broth:

Ingredients:

- 6 cups chicken or vegetable broth
- 2 cups water
- 3-4 cloves garlic, minced
- 1-inch piece of ginger, sliced
- 2 tablespoons soy sauce
- 2 tablespoons mirin (Japanese sweet rice wine)
- 1 tablespoon sesame oil
- 1 tablespoon chili oil (adjust to taste)
- 2-3 tablespoons spicy miso paste (adjust to taste)
- Salt and pepper to taste

Instructions:

1. **Prepare the broth:** In a large pot, combine chicken or vegetable broth, water, minced garlic, ginger slices, soy sauce, mirin, sesame oil, and chili oil. Bring to a boil.
2. **Simmer:** Reduce heat and simmer for about 15-20 minutes to allow flavors to meld together.
3. **Add miso paste:** Stir in spicy miso paste until dissolved. Taste and adjust seasoning with salt, pepper, or more miso paste as desired. Keep the broth warm while preparing other components.

Noodles:

Ingredients:

- Fresh ramen noodles (or dried if fresh are unavailable)
- Water for boiling

Instructions:

1. **Cook the noodles:** Boil water in a separate pot and cook the ramen noodles according to package instructions (usually about 1-2 minutes for fresh noodles).
2. **Drain and rinse:** Drain the noodles and rinse under cold water to stop the cooking process. This helps maintain a firm texture.

Toppings:

- Thinly sliced chashu pork or chicken (can also use tofu for vegetarian option)
- Soft-boiled eggs, halved
- Bamboo shoots (menma)

- Nori (seaweed sheets), sliced into strips
- Green onions, finely chopped
- Corn kernels (optional)
- Bean sprouts (optional)
- Toasted sesame seeds (optional)

Assembly:

1. **Prepare bowls:** Divide cooked noodles among serving bowls.
2. **Add toppings:** Arrange chashu pork or chicken slices, soft-boiled egg halves, bamboo shoots, nori strips, green onions, and any other desired toppings over the noodles.
3. **Pour broth:** Ladle hot spicy miso broth over the noodles and toppings.
4. **Serve immediately:** Garnish with toasted sesame seeds if using, and serve your Spicy Miso Ramen piping hot!

Feel free to adjust the spiciness level by adding more or less chili oil and spicy miso paste according to your preference. This recipe provides a deliciously hearty and spicy bowl of ramen that's perfect for any ramen enthusiast!

Shoyu Ramen

Broth:

Ingredients:

- 6 cups chicken or vegetable broth
- 2 cups water
- 3-4 cloves garlic, minced
- 1-inch piece of ginger, sliced
- 2 tablespoons soy sauce
- 1 tablespoon mirin (Japanese sweet rice wine)
- 1 tablespoon sake (optional)
- 1 teaspoon sesame oil
- Salt and pepper to taste

Instructions:

1. **Prepare the broth:** In a large pot, combine chicken or vegetable broth, water, minced garlic, ginger slices, soy sauce, mirin, sake (if using), and sesame oil. Bring to a boil.
2. **Simmer:** Reduce heat and simmer for about 15-20 minutes to allow flavors to meld together.
3. **Season:** Taste and adjust seasoning with salt and pepper as needed. Keep the broth warm while preparing other components.

Noodles:

Ingredients:

- Fresh ramen noodles (or dried if fresh are unavailable)
- Water for boiling

Instructions:

1. **Cook the noodles:** Boil water in a separate pot and cook the ramen noodles according to package instructions (usually about 1-2 minutes for fresh noodles).
2. **Drain and rinse:** Drain the noodles and rinse under cold water to stop the cooking process. This helps maintain a firm texture.

Toppings:

- Thinly sliced chashu pork or chicken (can also use tofu for vegetarian option)
- Soft-boiled eggs, halved
- Bamboo shoots (menma)
- Nori (seaweed sheets), sliced into strips
- Green onions, finely chopped
- Naruto (fish cake slices)
- Corn kernels (optional)

- Bean sprouts (optional)
- Toasted sesame seeds (optional)

Assembly:

1. **Prepare bowls:** Divide cooked noodles among serving bowls.
2. **Add toppings:** Arrange chashu pork or chicken slices, soft-boiled egg halves, bamboo shoots, nori strips, green onions, naruto, and any other desired toppings over the noodles.
3. **Pour broth:** Ladle hot Shoyu broth over the noodles and toppings.
4. **Serve immediately:** Garnish with toasted sesame seeds if using, and serve your Shoyu Ramen piping hot!

This recipe provides a delicious and savory bowl of Shoyu Ramen that's perfect for enjoying homemade Japanese comfort food. Adjust the toppings and seasonings according to your taste preferences for a personalized ramen experience.

Vegetarian Ramen

Broth:

Ingredients:

- 6 cups vegetable broth
- 2 cups water
- 3-4 cloves garlic, minced
- 1-inch piece of ginger, sliced
- 2 tablespoons soy sauce (or tamari for gluten-free option)
- 1 tablespoon miso paste (white or yellow)
- 1 tablespoon mirin (Japanese sweet rice wine)
- 1 teaspoon sesame oil
- Salt and pepper to taste

Instructions:

1. **Prepare the broth:** In a large pot, combine vegetable broth, water, minced garlic, ginger slices, soy sauce, miso paste, mirin, and sesame oil. Bring to a boil.
2. **Simmer:** Reduce heat and simmer for about 15-20 minutes to allow flavors to meld together.
3. **Season:** Taste and adjust seasoning with salt and pepper as needed. Keep the broth warm while preparing other components.

Noodles:

Ingredients:

- Fresh ramen noodles (or dried if fresh are unavailable)
- Water for boiling

Instructions:

1. **Cook the noodles:** Boil water in a separate pot and cook the ramen noodles according to package instructions (usually about 1-2 minutes for fresh noodles).
2. **Drain and rinse:** Drain the noodles and rinse under cold water to stop the cooking process. This helps maintain a firm texture.

Toppings:

- Pan-fried tofu, sliced into cubes or strips
- Soft-boiled eggs (omit for vegan option)
- Bamboo shoots (menma)
- Nori (seaweed sheets), sliced into strips
- Green onions, finely chopped

- Corn kernels
- Bean sprouts
- Shiitake mushrooms, sliced and sautéed
- Spinach or other leafy greens, blanched

Assembly:

1. **Prepare bowls:** Divide cooked noodles among serving bowls.
2. **Add toppings:** Arrange pan-fried tofu, soft-boiled egg halves (if using), bamboo shoots, nori strips, green onions, corn kernels, bean sprouts, sautéed mushrooms, and any other desired toppings over the noodles.
3. **Pour broth:** Ladle hot Vegetarian broth over the noodles and toppings.
4. **Serve immediately:** Garnish with additional green onions or sesame seeds if desired, and serve your Vegetarian Ramen piping hot!

This recipe provides a delicious and hearty bowl of Vegetarian Ramen that's packed with flavors and textures. Feel free to customize the toppings according to your preferences or what you have on hand. Enjoy your homemade vegetarian ramen!

Chicken Ramen

Broth:

Ingredients:

- 6 cups chicken broth
- 2 cups water
- 3-4 cloves garlic, minced
- 1-inch piece of ginger, sliced
- 2 tablespoons soy sauce
- 1 tablespoon mirin (Japanese sweet rice wine)
- 1 teaspoon sesame oil
- Salt and pepper to taste

Instructions:

1. **Prepare the broth:** In a large pot, combine chicken broth, water, minced garlic, ginger slices, soy sauce, mirin, and sesame oil. Bring to a boil.
2. **Simmer:** Reduce heat and simmer for about 15-20 minutes to allow flavors to meld together.
3. **Season:** Taste and adjust seasoning with salt and pepper as needed. Keep the broth warm while preparing other components.

Noodles:

Ingredients:

- Fresh ramen noodles (or dried if fresh are unavailable)
- Water for boiling

Instructions:

1. **Cook the noodles:** Boil water in a separate pot and cook the ramen noodles according to package instructions (usually about 1-2 minutes for fresh noodles).
2. **Drain and rinse:** Drain the noodles and rinse under cold water to stop the cooking process. This helps maintain a firm texture.

Chicken:

Ingredients:

- 2 boneless, skinless chicken breasts
- Salt and pepper
- 1 tablespoon vegetable oil

Instructions:

1. **Cook the chicken:** Season chicken breasts with salt and pepper. In a skillet over medium-high heat, heat vegetable oil. Cook chicken breasts for about 6-7 minutes per side until fully cooked and internal temperature reaches 165°F (75°C). Remove from heat and let rest for a few minutes before slicing thinly.

Toppings:

- Sliced cooked chicken (from above)
- Soft-boiled eggs, halved
- Bamboo shoots (menma)
- Nori (seaweed sheets), sliced into strips
- Green onions, finely chopped
- Corn kernels (optional)
- Bean sprouts (optional)
- Toasted sesame seeds (optional)

Assembly:

1. **Prepare bowls:** Divide cooked noodles among serving bowls.
2. **Add toppings:** Arrange sliced cooked chicken, soft-boiled egg halves, bamboo shoots, nori strips, green onions, and any other desired toppings over the noodles.
3. **Pour broth:** Ladle hot Chicken broth over the noodles and toppings.
4. **Serve immediately:** Garnish with toasted sesame seeds if using, and serve your Chicken Ramen piping hot!

Feel free to customize your Chicken Ramen with additional toppings or adjust the seasoning of the broth to your taste. This recipe provides a comforting and satisfying bowl of Chicken Ramen that's perfect for any occasion. Enjoy!

Beef Ramen

Broth:

Ingredients:

- 6 cups beef broth
- 2 cups water
- 3-4 cloves garlic, minced
- 1-inch piece of ginger, sliced
- 2 tablespoons soy sauce
- 1 tablespoon mirin (Japanese sweet rice wine)
- 1 tablespoon sake (optional)
- 1 teaspoon sesame oil
- Salt and pepper to taste

Instructions:

1. **Prepare the broth:** In a large pot, combine beef broth, water, minced garlic, ginger slices, soy sauce, mirin, sake (if using), and sesame oil. Bring to a boil.
2. **Simmer:** Reduce heat and simmer for about 15-20 minutes to allow flavors to meld together.
3. **Season:** Taste and adjust seasoning with salt and pepper as needed. Keep the broth warm while preparing other components.

Noodles:

Ingredients:

- Fresh ramen noodles (or dried if fresh are unavailable)
- Water for boiling

Instructions:

1. **Cook the noodles:** Boil water in a separate pot and cook the ramen noodles according to package instructions (usually about 1-2 minutes for fresh noodles).
2. **Drain and rinse:** Drain the noodles and rinse under cold water to stop the cooking process. This helps maintain a firm texture.

Beef:

Ingredients:

- 1/2 pound beef (sirloin, flank, or any tender cut), thinly sliced
- Salt and pepper
- 1 tablespoon vegetable oil

1. **Cook the chicken:** Season chicken breasts with salt and pepper. In a skillet over medium-high heat, heat vegetable oil. Cook chicken breasts for about 6-7 minutes per side until fully cooked and internal temperature reaches 165°F (75°C). Remove from heat and let rest for a few minutes before slicing thinly.

Toppings:

- Sliced cooked chicken (from above)
- Soft-boiled eggs, halved
- Bamboo shoots (menma)
- Nori (seaweed sheets), sliced into strips
- Green onions, finely chopped
- Corn kernels (optional)
- Bean sprouts (optional)
- Toasted sesame seeds (optional)

Assembly:

1. **Prepare bowls:** Divide cooked noodles among serving bowls.
2. **Add toppings:** Arrange sliced cooked chicken, soft-boiled egg halves, bamboo shoots, nori strips, green onions, and any other desired toppings over the noodles.
3. **Pour broth:** Ladle hot Chicken broth over the noodles and toppings.
4. **Serve immediately:** Garnish with toasted sesame seeds if using, and serve your Chicken Ramen piping hot!

Feel free to customize your Chicken Ramen with additional toppings or adjust the seasoning of the broth to your taste. This recipe provides a comforting and satisfying bowl of Chicken Ramen that's perfect for any occasion. Enjoy!

Beef Ramen

Broth:

Ingredients:

- 6 cups beef broth
- 2 cups water
- 3-4 cloves garlic, minced
- 1-inch piece of ginger, sliced
- 2 tablespoons soy sauce
- 1 tablespoon mirin (Japanese sweet rice wine)
- 1 tablespoon sake (optional)
- 1 teaspoon sesame oil
- Salt and pepper to taste

Instructions:

1. **Prepare the broth:** In a large pot, combine beef broth, water, minced garlic, ginger slices, soy sauce, mirin, sake (if using), and sesame oil. Bring to a boil.
2. **Simmer:** Reduce heat and simmer for about 15-20 minutes to allow flavors to meld together.
3. **Season:** Taste and adjust seasoning with salt and pepper as needed. Keep the broth warm while preparing other components.

Noodles:

Ingredients:

- Fresh ramen noodles (or dried if fresh are unavailable)
- Water for boiling

Instructions:

1. **Cook the noodles:** Boil water in a separate pot and cook the ramen noodles according to package instructions (usually about 1-2 minutes for fresh noodles).
2. **Drain and rinse:** Drain the noodles and rinse under cold water to stop the cooking process. This helps maintain a firm texture.

Beef:

Ingredients:

- 1/2 pound beef (sirloin, flank, or any tender cut), thinly sliced
- Salt and pepper
- 1 tablespoon vegetable oil

Instructions:

1. **Cook the beef:** Season beef slices with salt and pepper. In a skillet or frying pan over medium-high heat, heat vegetable oil. Cook beef slices for about 1-2 minutes per side until browned and cooked to your liking. Remove from heat and set aside.

Toppings:

- Cooked beef slices (from above)
- Soft-boiled eggs, halved
- Bamboo shoots (menma)
- Nori (seaweed sheets), sliced into strips
- Green onions, finely chopped
- Corn kernels (optional)
- Bean sprouts (optional)
- Toasted sesame seeds (optional)

Assembly:

1. **Prepare bowls:** Divide cooked noodles among serving bowls.
2. **Add toppings:** Arrange cooked beef slices, soft-boiled egg halves, bamboo shoots, nori strips, green onions, and any other desired toppings over the noodles.
3. **Pour broth:** Ladle hot Beef broth over the noodles and toppings.
4. **Serve immediately:** Garnish with toasted sesame seeds if using, and serve your Beef Ramen piping hot!

Feel free to customize your Beef Ramen with additional toppings such as mushrooms, spinach, or other vegetables. Adjust the seasoning of the broth to your taste preferences for a comforting and delicious bowl of homemade Beef Ramen. Enjoy!

Seafood Ramen

Broth:

Ingredients:

- 6 cups seafood or fish broth (you can make your own by simmering fish bones and shrimp shells, or use store-bought)
- 2 cups water
- 3-4 cloves garlic, minced
- 1-inch piece of ginger, sliced
- 2 tablespoons soy sauce
- 1 tablespoon mirin (Japanese sweet rice wine)
- 1 tablespoon sake (optional)
- 1 teaspoon sesame oil
- Salt and pepper to taste

Instructions:

1. **Prepare the broth:** In a large pot, combine seafood or fish broth, water, minced garlic, ginger slices, soy sauce, mirin, sake (if using), and sesame oil. Bring to a boil.
2. **Simmer:** Reduce heat and simmer for about 15-20 minutes to allow flavors to meld together.
3. **Season:** Taste and adjust seasoning with salt and pepper as needed. Keep the broth warm while preparing other components.

Noodles:

Ingredients:

- Fresh ramen noodles (or dried if fresh are unavailable)
- Water for boiling

Instructions:

1. **Cook the noodles:** Boil water in a separate pot and cook the ramen noodles according to package instructions (usually about 1-2 minutes for fresh noodles).
2. **Drain and rinse:** Drain the noodles and rinse under cold water to stop the cooking process. This helps maintain a firm texture.

Seafood:

Ingredients:

- Assorted seafood such as shrimp, scallops, squid, mussels, etc.
- Salt and pepper

- 1 tablespoon vegetable oil

Instructions:

1. **Prepare the seafood:** Season seafood with salt and pepper. In a skillet or frying pan over medium-high heat, heat vegetable oil. Cook seafood for a few minutes until just cooked through and opaque. Remove from heat and set aside.

Toppings:

- Cooked seafood (from above)
- Soft-boiled eggs, halved
- Bamboo shoots (menma)
- Nori (seaweed sheets), sliced into strips
- Green onions, finely chopped
- Corn kernels (optional)
- Bean sprouts (optional)
- Toasted sesame seeds (optional)

Assembly:

1. **Prepare bowls:** Divide cooked noodles among serving bowls.
2. **Add toppings:** Arrange cooked seafood, soft-boiled egg halves, bamboo shoots, nori strips, green onions, and any other desired toppings over the noodles.
3. **Pour broth:** Ladle hot Seafood broth over the noodles and toppings.
4. **Serve immediately:** Garnish with toasted sesame seeds if using, and serve your Seafood Ramen piping hot!

Feel free to customize your Seafood Ramen with additional seafood or vegetables like spinach or bok choy. Adjust the seasoning of the broth to your taste preferences for a delicious and comforting bowl of homemade Seafood Ramen. Enjoy!

Kimchi Ramen

Broth:

Ingredients:

- 6 cups chicken or vegetable broth
- 2 cups water
- 1 cup kimchi, chopped
- 3-4 cloves garlic, minced
- 1-inch piece of ginger, sliced
- 2 tablespoons soy sauce
- 1 tablespoon sesame oil
- 1 tablespoon gochujang (Korean red chili paste)
- Salt and pepper to taste

Instructions:

1. **Prepare the broth:** In a large pot, combine chicken or vegetable broth, water, chopped kimchi (including the juice), minced garlic, ginger slices, soy sauce, sesame oil, and gochujang. Bring to a boil.
2. **Simmer:** Reduce heat and simmer for about 15-20 minutes to allow flavors to meld together.
3. **Season:** Taste and adjust seasoning with salt and pepper as needed. Keep the broth warm while preparing other components.

Noodles:

Ingredients:

- Fresh ramen noodles (or dried if fresh are unavailable)
- Water for boiling

Instructions:

1. **Cook the noodles:** Boil water in a separate pot and cook the ramen noodles according to package instructions (usually about 1-2 minutes for fresh noodles).
2. **Drain and rinse:** Drain the noodles and rinse under cold water to stop the cooking process. This helps maintain a firm texture.

Toppings:

- Sliced pork belly or chicken (optional)
- Soft-boiled eggs, halved
- Kimchi (additional for topping)
- Nori (seaweed sheets), sliced into strips

- Green onions, finely chopped
- Sesame seeds, toasted
- Bean sprouts (optional)

Assembly:

1. **Prepare bowls:** Divide cooked noodles among serving bowls.
2. **Add toppings:** Arrange sliced pork belly or chicken (if using), soft-boiled egg halves, kimchi, nori strips, green onions, sesame seeds, and any other desired toppings over the noodles.
3. **Pour broth:** Ladle hot Kimchi broth over the noodles and toppings.
4. **Serve immediately:** Garnish with additional kimchi or sesame seeds if desired, and serve your Kimchi Ramen piping hot!

This recipe provides a delicious and spicy bowl of Kimchi Ramen that's full of robust flavors. Adjust the spiciness level by adding more or less gochujang according to your preference. Enjoy your homemade Kimchi Ramen!

Vegan Miso Ramen

Broth:

Ingredients:

- 6 cups vegetable broth
- 2 cups water
- 3-4 cloves garlic, minced
- 1-inch piece of ginger, sliced
- 1/4 cup miso paste (white or yellow)
- 2 tablespoons soy sauce (or tamari for gluten-free option)
- 1 tablespoon sesame oil
- 1 tablespoon mirin (Japanese sweet rice wine)
- Salt and pepper to taste

Instructions:

1. **Prepare the broth:** In a large pot, combine vegetable broth, water, minced garlic, ginger slices, miso paste, soy sauce, sesame oil, and mirin. Bring to a boil.
2. **Simmer:** Reduce heat and simmer for about 15-20 minutes to allow flavors to meld together.
3. **Season:** Taste and adjust seasoning with salt and pepper as needed. Keep the broth warm while preparing other components.

Noodles:

Ingredients:

- Fresh ramen noodles (or dried if fresh are unavailable)
- Water for boiling

Instructions:

1. **Cook the noodles:** Boil water in a separate pot and cook the ramen noodles according to package instructions (usually about 1-2 minutes for fresh noodles).
2. **Drain and rinse:** Drain the noodles and rinse under cold water to stop the cooking process. This helps maintain a firm texture.

Toppings:

- Pan-fried tofu, sliced into cubes or strips
- Sautéed mushrooms (shiitake, oyster, or your choice)
- Bamboo shoots (menma)
- Nori (seaweed sheets), sliced into strips
- Green onions, finely chopped

- Bean sprouts
- Corn kernels (optional)
- Sesame seeds, toasted

Assembly:

1. **Prepare bowls:** Divide cooked noodles among serving bowls.
2. **Add toppings:** Arrange pan-fried tofu, sautéed mushrooms, bamboo shoots, nori strips, green onions, bean sprouts, corn kernels, and any other desired toppings over the noodles.
3. **Pour broth:** Ladle hot Vegan Miso broth over the noodles and toppings.
4. **Serve immediately:** Garnish with toasted sesame seeds if using, and serve your Vegan Miso Ramen piping hot!

Feel free to customize your Vegan Miso Ramen with additional vegetables like spinach or bok choy. Adjust the thickness and saltiness of the broth by adding more or less miso paste. This recipe provides a delicious and satisfying bowl of Vegan Miso Ramen that's perfect for any occasion. Enjoy!

Pork Belly Ramen

Broth:

Ingredients:

- 6 cups chicken or pork broth
- 2 cups water
- 3-4 cloves garlic, minced
- 1-inch piece of ginger, sliced
- 2 tablespoons soy sauce
- 1 tablespoon mirin (Japanese sweet rice wine)
- 1 tablespoon sake (optional)
- 1 teaspoon sesame oil
- Salt and pepper to taste

Instructions:

1. **Prepare the broth:** In a large pot, combine chicken or pork broth, water, minced garlic, ginger slices, soy sauce, mirin, sake (if using), and sesame oil. Bring to a boil.
2. **Simmer:** Reduce heat and simmer for about 15-20 minutes to allow flavors to meld together.
3. **Season:** Taste and adjust seasoning with salt and pepper as needed. Keep the broth warm while preparing other components.

Pork Belly:

Ingredients:

- 1 pound pork belly, skin removed and cut into thick slices
- Salt and pepper
- 1 tablespoon vegetable oil

Instructions:

1. **Cook the pork belly:** Season pork belly slices with salt and pepper. In a skillet or frying pan over medium-high heat, heat vegetable oil. Cook pork belly slices for about 3-4 minutes per side until browned and crispy. Remove from heat and set aside on paper towels to drain excess oil. Slice thinly before serving.

Noodles:

Ingredients:

- Fresh ramen noodles (or dried if fresh are unavailable)
- Water for boiling

Instructions:

1. **Cook the noodles:** Boil water in a separate pot and cook the ramen noodles according to package instructions (usually about 1-2 minutes for fresh noodles).
2. **Drain and rinse:** Drain the noodles and rinse under cold water to stop the cooking process. This helps maintain a firm texture.

Toppings:

- Soft-boiled eggs, halved
- Bamboo shoots (menma)
- Nori (seaweed sheets), sliced into strips
- Green onions, finely chopped
- Bean sprouts
- Corn kernels (optional)
- Sesame seeds, toasted

Assembly:

1. **Prepare bowls:** Divide cooked noodles among serving bowls.
2. **Add toppings:** Arrange sliced pork belly, soft-boiled egg halves, bamboo shoots, nori strips, green onions, bean sprouts, corn kernels, and any other desired toppings over the noodles.
3. **Pour broth:** Ladle hot Pork Belly broth over the noodles and toppings.
4. **Serve immediately:** Garnish with toasted sesame seeds if using, and serve your Pork Belly Ramen piping hot!

This recipe provides a delicious and indulgent bowl of Pork Belly Ramen that's sure to satisfy. Adjust the richness of the broth and the amount of toppings according to your preferences for a personalized ramen experience. Enjoy!

Garlic Sesame Ramen

Broth:

Ingredients:

- 6 cups chicken or vegetable broth
- 2 cups water
- 6 cloves garlic, minced
- 1-inch piece of ginger, sliced
- 2 tablespoons soy sauce
- 1 tablespoon sesame oil
- 1 tablespoon mirin (Japanese sweet rice wine)
- 1 teaspoon rice vinegar
- Salt and pepper to taste

Instructions:

1. **Prepare the broth:** In a large pot, combine chicken or vegetable broth, water, minced garlic, ginger slices, soy sauce, sesame oil, mirin, and rice vinegar. Bring to a boil.
2. **Simmer:** Reduce heat and simmer for about 15-20 minutes to allow flavors to meld together.
3. **Season:** Taste and adjust seasoning with salt and pepper as needed. Keep the broth warm while preparing other components.

Noodles:

Ingredients:

- Fresh ramen noodles (or dried if fresh are unavailable)
- Water for boiling

Instructions:

1. **Cook the noodles:** Boil water in a separate pot and cook the ramen noodles according to package instructions (usually about 1-2 minutes for fresh noodles).
2. **Drain and rinse:** Drain the noodles and rinse under cold water to stop the cooking process. This helps maintain a firm texture.

Toppings:

- Pan-fried tofu, sliced into cubes or strips
- Soft-boiled eggs, halved
- Baby spinach or other leafy greens
- Bamboo shoots (menma)
- Nori (seaweed sheets), sliced into strips

- Green onions, finely chopped
- Toasted sesame seeds
- Red pepper flakes (optional for added spice)

Assembly:

1. **Prepare bowls:** Divide cooked noodles among serving bowls.
2. **Add toppings:** Arrange pan-fried tofu, soft-boiled egg halves, baby spinach, bamboo shoots, nori strips, green onions, toasted sesame seeds, and red pepper flakes (if using) over the noodles.
3. **Pour broth:** Ladle hot Garlic Sesame broth over the noodles and toppings.
4. **Serve immediately:** Garnish with extra sesame seeds and green onions if desired, and serve your Garlic Sesame Ramen piping hot!

This recipe offers a comforting and flavorful bowl of ramen with a delightful garlic and sesame twist. Adjust the amount of garlic and sesame oil according to your taste preferences. Enjoy your homemade Garlic Sesame Ramen!

Curry Ramen

Broth:

Ingredients:

- 6 cups chicken or vegetable broth
- 2 cups water
- 3-4 cloves garlic, minced
- 1-inch piece of ginger, sliced
- 2 tablespoons soy sauce
- 1 tablespoon sesame oil
- 1 tablespoon curry powder (adjust to taste)
- 1 tablespoon miso paste (optional, for added depth)
- Salt and pepper to taste

Instructions:

1. **Prepare the broth:** In a large pot, combine chicken or vegetable broth, water, minced garlic, ginger slices, soy sauce, sesame oil, curry powder, and miso paste (if using). Bring to a boil.
2. **Simmer:** Reduce heat and simmer for about 15-20 minutes to allow flavors to meld together.
3. **Season:** Taste and adjust seasoning with salt and pepper as needed. Keep the broth warm while preparing other components.

Noodles:

Ingredients:

- Fresh ramen noodles (or dried if fresh are unavailable)
- Water for boiling

Instructions:

1. **Cook the noodles:** Boil water in a separate pot and cook the ramen noodles according to package instructions (usually about 1-2 minutes for fresh noodles).
2. **Drain and rinse:** Drain the noodles and rinse under cold water to stop the cooking process. This helps maintain a firm texture.

Toppings:

- Sliced cooked chicken or pork (optional)
- Soft-boiled eggs, halved
- Bamboo shoots (menma)
- Nori (seaweed sheets), sliced into strips

- Green onions, finely chopped
- Bean sprouts
- Corn kernels (optional)
- Red chili flakes (optional for added spice)

Assembly:

1. **Prepare bowls:** Divide cooked noodles among serving bowls.
2. **Add toppings:** Arrange sliced cooked meat (if using), soft-boiled egg halves, bamboo shoots, nori strips, green onions, bean sprouts, corn kernels, and any other desired toppings over the noodles.
3. **Pour broth:** Ladle hot Curry broth over the noodles and toppings.
4. **Serve immediately:** Garnish with red chili flakes if desired, and serve your Curry Ramen piping hot!

Feel free to adjust the spiciness and richness of the broth by varying the amount of curry powder and miso paste. This recipe provides a delicious fusion of Japanese ramen and curry flavors that's perfect for warming up on a chilly day. Enjoy your homemade Curry Ramen!

Creamy Chicken Ramen

Broth:

Ingredients:

- 6 cups chicken broth
- 2 cups water
- 3-4 cloves garlic, minced
- 1-inch piece of ginger, sliced
- 1 tablespoon soy sauce
- 1 tablespoon miso paste (white or yellow)
- 1 tablespoon sesame oil
- 1/2 cup heavy cream or coconut cream (for a dairy-free option)
- Salt and pepper to taste

Instructions:

1. **Prepare the broth:** In a large pot, combine chicken broth, water, minced garlic, ginger slices, soy sauce, miso paste, and sesame oil. Bring to a boil.
2. **Simmer:** Reduce heat and simmer for about 15-20 minutes to allow flavors to meld together.
3. **Add cream:** Stir in heavy cream or coconut cream, and continue to simmer for another 5 minutes. Adjust the thickness of the broth by adding more cream if desired. Season with salt and pepper to taste.
4. **Keep warm:** Keep the creamy broth warm while preparing other components.

Noodles:

Ingredients:

- Fresh ramen noodles (or dried if fresh are unavailable)
- Water for boiling

Instructions:

1. **Cook the noodles:** Boil water in a separate pot and cook the ramen noodles according to package instructions (usually about 1-2 minutes for fresh noodles).
2. **Drain and rinse:** Drain the noodles and rinse under cold water to stop the cooking process. This helps maintain a firm texture.

Chicken:

Ingredients:

- 2 boneless, skinless chicken breasts

- Salt and pepper
- 1 tablespoon vegetable oil

Instructions:

1. **Cook the chicken:** Season chicken breasts with salt and pepper. In a skillet over medium-high heat, heat vegetable oil. Cook chicken breasts for about 6-7 minutes per side until fully cooked and internal temperature reaches 165°F (75°C). Remove from heat and let rest for a few minutes before slicing thinly.

Toppings:

- Sliced cooked chicken (from above)
- Soft-boiled eggs, halved
- Bamboo shoots (menma)
- Nori (seaweed sheets), sliced into strips
- Green onions, finely chopped
- Corn kernels (optional)
- Bean sprouts (optional)
- Toasted sesame seeds (optional)

Assembly:

1. **Prepare bowls:** Divide cooked noodles among serving bowls.
2. **Add toppings:** Arrange sliced cooked chicken, soft-boiled egg halves, bamboo shoots, nori strips, green onions, corn kernels, bean sprouts, and any other desired toppings over the noodles.
3. **Pour creamy broth:** Ladle hot Creamy Chicken broth over the noodles and toppings.
4. **Serve immediately:** Garnish with toasted sesame seeds if using, and serve your Creamy Chicken Ramen piping hot!

This recipe provides a comforting and creamy bowl of ramen that's perfect for indulging in. Customize your toppings and adjust the creaminess of the broth to your taste preferences. Enjoy your homemade Creamy Chicken Ramen!

Thai Coconut Ramen

Broth:

Ingredients:

- 6 cups vegetable broth
- 2 cups coconut milk (full-fat for creaminess)
- 3-4 cloves garlic, minced
- 1-inch piece of ginger, sliced
- 2 tablespoons soy sauce (or tamari for gluten-free)
- 2 tablespoons Thai red curry paste
- 1 tablespoon brown sugar
- 1 tablespoon lime juice
- Salt and pepper to taste

Instructions:

1. **Prepare the broth:** In a large pot, combine vegetable broth, coconut milk, minced garlic, ginger slices, soy sauce, Thai red curry paste, brown sugar, and lime juice. Bring to a boil.
2. **Simmer:** Reduce heat and simmer for about 15-20 minutes to allow flavors to meld together.
3. **Season:** Taste and adjust seasoning with salt and pepper as needed. Keep the broth warm while preparing other components.

Noodles:

Ingredients:

- Fresh ramen noodles (or dried if fresh are unavailable)
- Water for boiling

Instructions:

1. **Cook the noodles:** Boil water in a separate pot and cook the ramen noodles according to package instructions (usually about 1-2 minutes for fresh noodles).
2. **Drain and rinse:** Drain the noodles and rinse under cold water to stop the cooking process. This helps maintain a firm texture.

Toppings:

- Sliced cooked chicken, shrimp, or tofu (optional)
- Fresh vegetables such as bell peppers, snow peas, or baby corn
- Bean sprouts
- Fresh cilantro leaves

- Lime wedges
- Thai basil leaves (optional)
- Red chili flakes (optional for added spice)

Assembly:

1. **Prepare bowls:** Divide cooked noodles among serving bowls.
2. **Add toppings:** Arrange sliced cooked protein (if using), fresh vegetables, bean sprouts, cilantro leaves, lime wedges, Thai basil leaves, and any other desired toppings over the noodles.
3. **Pour coconut broth:** Ladle hot Thai Coconut broth over the noodles and toppings.
4. **Serve immediately:** Garnish with red chili flakes if desired, and serve your Thai Coconut Ramen piping hot!

This recipe provides a delightful fusion of ramen and Thai flavors, creating a creamy and aromatic noodle soup that's both comforting and exotic. Adjust the spiciness and sweetness of the broth according to your taste preferences. Enjoy your homemade Thai Coconut Ramen!

Ramen Carbonara

Ingredients:

- 2 packs of instant ramen noodles (discard seasoning packets)
- 200g pancetta or bacon, diced
- 3 cloves garlic, minced
- 2 large eggs
- 1/2 cup grated Parmesan cheese, plus extra for garnish
- Salt and black pepper to taste
- Chopped fresh parsley for garnish

Instructions:

1. **Cook Ramen Noodles:**
   - Bring a large pot of water to a boil. Cook the ramen noodles according to package instructions until al dente. Drain and set aside.
2. **Prepare Carbonara Sauce:**
   - In a large skillet or frying pan, cook the diced pancetta or bacon over medium heat until crispy. Remove from pan and set aside on a paper towel-lined plate to drain excess fat.
   - In the same skillet with the rendered fat, add minced garlic and cook for about 1 minute until fragrant.
3. **Make Carbonara Mixture:**
   - In a bowl, whisk together the eggs and grated Parmesan cheese until smooth.
4. **Combine Noodles and Sauce:**
   - Add the cooked and drained ramen noodles to the skillet with the garlic. Toss to coat the noodles with the garlic-infused fat.
   - Remove the skillet from heat and quickly pour the egg and Parmesan mixture over the noodles, stirring continuously to coat the noodles evenly. The residual heat from the noodles will cook the eggs and create a creamy sauce.
   - Season with salt and black pepper to taste.
5. **Serve:**
   - Divide the Ramen Carbonara among serving bowls.
   - Top each bowl with crispy pancetta or bacon.
   - Garnish with extra grated Parmesan cheese, chopped fresh parsley, and a sprinkle of black pepper.
6. **Enjoy:**
   - Serve immediately while hot and enjoy the creamy, comforting flavors of Ramen Carbonara!

This recipe offers a delightful twist on both Italian and Japanese cuisines, creating a satisfying and creamy noodle dish that's perfect for a cozy meal at home. Adjust the seasoning and cheese to your taste preferences for a personalized Ramen Carbonara experience.

Ramen with Poached Egg

Ingredients:

- 2 packs of instant ramen noodles (discard seasoning packets)
- 4 cups water
- 2 eggs
- 2 tablespoons soy sauce
- 1 tablespoon sesame oil
- 1 teaspoon rice vinegar (optional)
- Salt and pepper to taste
- Thinly sliced green onions (optional, for garnish)
- Nori (seaweed sheets), sliced into strips (optional, for garnish)
- Toasted sesame seeds (optional, for garnish)

Instructions:

1. **Prepare Ramen Noodles:**
    - Bring 4 cups of water to a boil in a large pot. Add the ramen noodles and cook according to package instructions until al dente. Drain and set aside.
2. **Poach Eggs:**
    - While the noodles are cooking, prepare the poached eggs. Bring a separate pot of water to a gentle simmer (not boiling). Add a teaspoon of vinegar to the water (optional, helps the eggs stay together).
    - Crack each egg into a small bowl or ramekin. Create a gentle whirlpool in the simmering water using a spoon, then carefully slide each egg into the center of the whirlpool.
    - Poach the eggs for about 3-4 minutes until the whites are set but the yolks are still runny. Use a slotted spoon to remove the poached eggs and place them on a plate lined with paper towels to drain excess water.
3. **Assemble Ramen Bowls:**
    - Divide the cooked ramen noodles into serving bowls.
    - Pour soy sauce and sesame oil over the noodles, and gently toss to coat evenly.
4. **Add Poached Eggs:**
    - Carefully place a poached egg on top of each bowl of noodles.
5. **Season and Garnish:**
    - Season the ramen with salt and pepper to taste.
    - Garnish with thinly sliced green onions, nori strips, and toasted sesame seeds if desired.
6. **Serve:**
    - Serve the Ramen with Poached Egg immediately while hot, allowing the yolk to mix with the noodles for a creamy texture and rich flavor.

This recipe provides a comforting and satisfying meal that's perfect for any time of day. The poached egg adds a luxurious touch to the simple ramen noodles, creating a dish that's both comforting and nutritious. Enjoy your homemade Ramen with Poached Egg!

Ramen with Grilled Tofu

Ingredients:

- 2 packs of instant ramen noodles (discard seasoning packets)
- 4 cups vegetable broth or water
- 1 block (14-16 oz) firm tofu
- 2 tablespoons soy sauce
- 1 tablespoon sesame oil
- 1 tablespoon rice vinegar (optional)
- 2 cloves garlic, minced
- 1-inch piece of ginger, grated
- Salt and pepper to taste
- Thinly sliced green onions, for garnish
- Sesame seeds, toasted, for garnish
- Nori (seaweed sheets), sliced into strips, for garnish (optional)

Instructions:

1. **Prepare Tofu:**
   - Drain the tofu and press it to remove excess water. Cut the tofu into slices or cubes, about 1/2 inch thick.
   - In a bowl, combine soy sauce, sesame oil, minced garlic, grated ginger, and rice vinegar (if using). Marinate the tofu in this mixture for at least 15-20 minutes to allow flavors to infuse.
2. **Grill Tofu:**
   - Heat a grill pan or skillet over medium-high heat. Brush with a little oil to prevent sticking.
   - Grill the marinated tofu slices or cubes for about 3-4 minutes on each side, or until nicely charred and heated through. Remove from heat and set aside.
3. **Cook Ramen Noodles:**
   - In a separate pot, bring vegetable broth or water to a boil.
   - Add the ramen noodles and cook according to package instructions until al dente. Drain and set aside.
4. **Assemble Ramen Bowls:**
   - Divide the cooked ramen noodles into serving bowls.
   - Pour the hot vegetable broth over the noodles.
5. **Add Grilled Tofu:**
   - Arrange grilled tofu slices or cubes on top of each bowl of ramen.
6. **Season and Garnish:**
   - Season the ramen with salt and pepper to taste.
   - Garnish with thinly sliced green onions, toasted sesame seeds, and nori strips (if using).
7. **Serve:**

- Serve the Ramen with Grilled Tofu immediately while hot, allowing the flavors to meld together.

This recipe provides a delicious and nutritious meal that's packed with protein and flavor. The grilled tofu adds a smoky and savory element to the ramen noodles, making it a satisfying dish for lunch or dinner. Enjoy your homemade Ramen with Grilled Tofu!

Ramen Stir-Fry

Ingredients:

- 2 packs of instant ramen noodles (discard seasoning packets)
- 1 tablespoon vegetable oil
- 1 block (14-16 oz) firm tofu, chicken, shrimp, or beef, diced (choose based on preference)
- 2 cups mixed vegetables (such as bell peppers, broccoli, carrots, snap peas, mushrooms, etc.), chopped
- 3 cloves garlic, minced
- 1-inch piece of ginger, grated
- 2 tablespoons soy sauce (or tamari for gluten-free)
- 1 tablespoon oyster sauce (optional)
- 1 tablespoon hoisin sauce (optional)
- 1 tablespoon sesame oil
- 1 teaspoon rice vinegar (optional)
- Salt and pepper to taste
- Thinly sliced green onions, for garnish
- Sesame seeds, toasted, for garnish (optional)

Instructions:

1. **Cook Ramen Noodles:**
   - Cook the ramen noodles in a pot of boiling water according to package instructions until al dente. Drain and set aside.
2. **Prepare Protein (Tofu or Meat):**
   - Heat vegetable oil in a large skillet or wok over medium-high heat.
   - Add diced tofu, chicken, shrimp, or beef to the skillet. Cook until browned and cooked through. Remove from skillet and set aside.
3. **Stir-Fry Vegetables:**
   - In the same skillet or wok, add a little more oil if needed. Add minced garlic and grated ginger, and sauté for about 1 minute until fragrant.
   - Add chopped mixed vegetables to the skillet. Stir-fry for 3-4 minutes until vegetables are tender-crisp.
4. **Make Stir-Fry Sauce:**
   - In a small bowl, whisk together soy sauce, oyster sauce (if using), hoisin sauce (if using), sesame oil, and rice vinegar (if using).
5. **Combine Noodles and Sauce:**
   - Add the cooked ramen noodles and the prepared stir-fry sauce to the skillet with the vegetables. Toss everything together until well combined and heated through.
6. **Add Protein:**
   - Return the cooked tofu, chicken, shrimp, or beef to the skillet. Stir to combine with the noodles and vegetables.
7. **Season and Garnish:**

- Taste and adjust seasoning with salt and pepper if needed.
- Garnish with thinly sliced green onions and toasted sesame seeds (if using).

8. **Serve:**
   - Divide the Ramen Stir-Fry among serving plates or bowls.
   - Serve hot and enjoy your homemade Ramen Stir-Fry!

This recipe is versatile, allowing you to customize the protein and vegetables based on your preferences or what you have on hand. The stir-fry sauce adds a delicious savory flavor to the dish, making it a satisfying and easy-to-make meal for lunch or dinner.

Ramen Salad

Ingredients:

- 2 packs of instant ramen noodles (discard seasoning packets)
- 1/2 head of cabbage, thinly shredded
- 1 cup shredded carrots
- 1/2 cup thinly sliced red bell pepper
- 1/2 cup thinly sliced cucumber
- 1/4 cup chopped green onions
- 1/4 cup sliced almonds or toasted sesame seeds (optional, for garnish)

Dressing:

- 1/4 cup vegetable oil
- 2 tablespoons rice vinegar
- 2 tablespoons soy sauce (or tamari for gluten-free)
- 1 tablespoon honey or brown sugar
- 1 teaspoon sesame oil
- 1 clove garlic, minced
- 1 teaspoon grated ginger
- Salt and pepper to taste

Instructions:

1. **Prepare Ramen Noodles:**
    - Crush the instant ramen noodles into small pieces. You can do this by placing the noodles in a plastic bag and gently crushing them with a rolling pin or your hands.
    - Heat a skillet over medium heat and toast the crushed ramen noodles (without seasoning packets) until golden brown and crispy. Set aside to cool.
2. **Make Dressing:**
    - In a small bowl, whisk together vegetable oil, rice vinegar, soy sauce, honey or brown sugar, sesame oil, minced garlic, grated ginger, salt, and pepper. Set aside.
3. **Assemble Salad:**
    - In a large mixing bowl, combine shredded cabbage, shredded carrots, sliced red bell pepper, sliced cucumber, and chopped green onions.
    - Add the toasted ramen noodles (reserve a handful for garnish) to the bowl with the vegetables.
4. **Toss with Dressing:**
    - Pour the prepared dressing over the salad ingredients.
    - Toss everything together until well combined and evenly coated with the dressing.
5. **Serve:**
    - Transfer the Ramen Salad to a serving dish or individual plates.

- Garnish with remaining toasted ramen noodles, sliced almonds or toasted sesame seeds (if using).
- Serve immediately as a refreshing side dish or light lunch.

This Ramen Salad is crunchy, flavorful, and packed with vegetables, making it a perfect dish for picnics, potlucks, or as a refreshing side to complement any meal. Enjoy the textures and flavors of this easy-to-make salad!

Ramen Burger

Ingredients:

- 2 packs of instant ramen noodles (discard seasoning packets)
- 1 pound ground beef (or ground chicken, turkey, or tofu for a vegetarian option)
- Salt and pepper to taste
- Vegetable oil, for cooking
- Cheese slices (optional)
- Lettuce leaves
- Sliced tomatoes
- Sliced onions
- Ketchup, mustard, or other condiments of choice

Instructions:

1. **Prepare Ramen Noodles:**
    - Cook the instant ramen noodles according to package instructions, but slightly undercook them to keep them firm. Drain and rinse the noodles under cold water to stop the cooking process. Let them cool slightly.
2. **Form Ramen Buns:**
    - Divide the cooked ramen noodles into four equal portions. Press each portion firmly into a round mold or shape them by hand into bun-sized patties (about 4-5 inches in diameter). Ensure the noodles are packed tightly together.
3. **Cook Ramen Buns:**
    - Heat a large non-stick skillet or griddle over medium heat. Brush lightly with vegetable oil.
    - Carefully transfer the formed ramen noodle buns to the skillet. Cook for about 3-4 minutes on each side until lightly golden and crispy. Press down gently with a spatula to flatten them slightly. Remove from heat and set aside.
4. **Prepare Burger Patties:**
    - Season the ground beef (or other protein) with salt and pepper. Divide into four equal portions and shape them into burger patties that are slightly larger than the diameter of the ramen buns.
5. **Cook Burger Patties:**
    - In the same skillet or griddle used for the ramen buns, cook the burger patties over medium-high heat for about 3-4 minutes per side, or until cooked to your desired doneness. If using cheese slices, place them on top of the patties during the last minute of cooking to melt.
6. **Assemble Ramen Burgers:**
    - Place a cooked ramen noodle bun on a serving plate. Top with lettuce leaves, a burger patty (with melted cheese if using), sliced tomatoes, and sliced onions.
    - Add condiments such as ketchup, mustard, or other sauces as desired.
7. **Serve:**
    - Top each assembled Ramen Burger with another ramen noodle bun.

- Serve immediately while hot and enjoy the unique and flavorful Ramen Burger!

This recipe allows for creativity in toppings and condiments, so feel free to customize your Ramen Burger with your favorite burger fixings. It's a fun and inventive way to enjoy both ramen and burgers in one delicious dish!

Ramen Pizza

Ingredients:

- 2 packs of instant ramen noodles (discard seasoning packets)
- 1 cup shredded mozzarella cheese
- 1/2 cup pizza sauce or marinara sauce
- 1/4 cup grated Parmesan cheese
- 1/2 cup sliced pepperoni or cooked sausage (optional)
- 1/4 cup sliced black olives (optional)
- 1/4 cup sliced mushrooms (optional)
- 1/4 cup sliced bell peppers (optional)
- Fresh basil leaves, chopped (optional)
- Red pepper flakes (optional, for spice)

Instructions:

1. **Prepare Ramen Noodles:**
    - Cook the instant ramen noodles according to package instructions, but slightly undercook them to keep them firm. Drain and rinse the noodles under cold water to stop the cooking process. Let them cool slightly.
2. **Form Ramen Crust:**
    - In a large mixing bowl, combine the cooked ramen noodles with 1/2 cup of shredded mozzarella cheese and grated Parmesan cheese. Mix well to coat the noodles evenly.
    - Press the ramen noodle mixture onto a pizza pan or baking sheet lined with parchment paper, forming it into a round shape to create the pizza crust. Press down firmly to compact the noodles.
3. **Bake Ramen Crust:**
    - Preheat your oven to 400°F (200°C).
    - Bake the ramen crust in the preheated oven for about 15-20 minutes, or until the edges are golden brown and crispy. Remove from oven and let it cool slightly.
4. **Assemble Ramen Pizza:**
    - Spread pizza sauce or marinara sauce evenly over the baked ramen crust, leaving a small border around the edges.
    - Sprinkle the remaining 1/2 cup of shredded mozzarella cheese over the sauce.
    - Add toppings such as sliced pepperoni, cooked sausage, black olives, sliced mushrooms, sliced bell peppers, and any other toppings of your choice.
5. **Bake Ramen Pizza:**
    - Return the assembled Ramen Pizza to the oven and bake for an additional 10-15 minutes, or until the cheese is melted and bubbly.
6. **Finish and Serve:**
    - Remove the Ramen Pizza from the oven and let it cool slightly before slicing.
    - Garnish with chopped fresh basil leaves and red pepper flakes if desired.

- Slice into wedges and serve hot as a unique and delicious twist on traditional pizza!

This recipe allows for customization with your favorite pizza toppings, making it a fun and creative dish to enjoy with family and friends. Experiment with different combinations to create your perfect Ramen Pizza!

Ramen Burrito

Ingredients:

- 2 packs of instant ramen noodles (discard seasoning packets)
- 1 cup shredded cooked chicken, beef, pork, tofu, or your choice of protein
- 1/2 cup cooked rice
- 1/2 cup shredded lettuce or cabbage
- 1/2 cup diced tomatoes
- 1/4 cup sliced avocado or guacamole
- 1/4 cup shredded cheese (cheddar, Monterey Jack, or your favorite)
- 1/4 cup sour cream or Greek yogurt
- Salsa or hot sauce (optional, for extra flavor)
- Flour tortillas (burrito-sized)

Instructions:

1. **Prepare Ramen Noodles:**
    - Cook the instant ramen noodles according to package instructions, but slightly undercook them to keep them firm. Drain and rinse the noodles under cold water to stop the cooking process. Let them cool slightly.
2. **Assemble Ramen Burrito:**
    - Lay a flour tortilla flat on a clean surface.
    - Spread a layer of cooked rice across the center of the tortilla.
    - Top with a layer of shredded lettuce or cabbage, diced tomatoes, sliced avocado or guacamole, and shredded cheese.
3. **Add Ramen Noodles and Protein:**
    - Place a portion of the cooked ramen noodles on top of the other ingredients in the tortilla.
    - Add shredded cooked chicken, beef, pork, tofu, or your choice of protein on top of the ramen noodles.
4. **Drizzle with Sauce:**
    - Drizzle sour cream or Greek yogurt over the filling ingredients.
    - Add salsa or hot sauce if desired for extra flavor.
5. **Roll Burrito:**
    - Fold the sides of the tortilla over the filling.
    - Roll the tortilla tightly from the bottom up to create a burrito shape, ensuring the filling is enclosed.
6. **Serve or Grill (Optional):**
    - Serve the Ramen Burrito immediately, or for a crispy exterior, heat a skillet over medium heat.
    - Lightly spray or brush the skillet with oil.
    - Place the burrito seam-side down and cook for 2-3 minutes on each side until golden brown and crispy.
7. **Slice and Enjoy:**

- Remove from the skillet and let it cool slightly before slicing.
- Slice the Ramen Burrito in half diagonally and serve hot.

This recipe offers a fun and inventive way to enjoy ramen noodles in a portable and satisfying format. Customize the ingredients to your taste preferences and enjoy your homemade Ramen Burrito!

Ramen Tacos

Ingredients:

- 2 packs of instant ramen noodles (discard seasoning packets)
- 1 pound ground beef, chicken, turkey, or tofu (choose based on preference)
- 1 tablespoon vegetable oil
- 1 packet taco seasoning mix (or homemade taco seasoning)
- 1/2 cup water
- Taco toppings:
    - Shredded lettuce
    - Diced tomatoes
    - Sliced avocado or guacamole
    - Shredded cheese (cheddar, Monterey Jack, or your favorite)
    - Sliced jalapeños (optional)
    - Chopped cilantro
    - Lime wedges
    - Salsa or hot sauce

Instructions:

1. **Prepare Ramen Noodles:**
    - Cook the instant ramen noodles according to package instructions, but slightly undercook them to keep them firm. Drain and rinse the noodles under cold water to stop the cooking process. Let them cool slightly.
2. **Cook Ground Meat or Tofu:**
    - Heat vegetable oil in a large skillet over medium-high heat.
    - Add ground meat or crumbled tofu to the skillet. Cook until browned and cooked through, breaking it up with a spoon as it cooks.
3. **Add Taco Seasoning:**
    - Sprinkle taco seasoning mix over the cooked meat or tofu. Stir to coat evenly.
4. **Add Water and Simmer:**
    - Pour 1/2 cup of water into the skillet with the seasoned meat or tofu. Stir well to combine.
    - Bring to a simmer and cook for about 5-7 minutes, stirring occasionally, until the sauce thickens and flavors meld together. Remove from heat and set aside.
5. **Prepare Ramen Taco Shells:**
    - While the meat or tofu is cooking, prepare the ramen taco shells. Divide the cooked ramen noodles into portions.
    - Press each portion into a round mold or shape them by hand into taco shell shapes, ensuring they are compact and hold their form.
6. **Bake Ramen Taco Shells (Optional):**
    - Preheat your oven to 400°F (200°C).
    - Place the shaped ramen taco shells on a baking sheet lined with parchment paper.

- Bake in the preheated oven for about 10-12 minutes, or until the edges are golden brown and crispy. Remove from oven and let them cool slightly.

7. **Assemble Ramen Tacos:**
    - Fill each ramen taco shell with the seasoned meat or tofu mixture.
    - Top with shredded lettuce, diced tomatoes, sliced avocado or guacamole, shredded cheese, sliced jalapeños (if using), chopped cilantro, and any other taco toppings of your choice.
8. **Serve:**
    - Serve the Ramen Tacos immediately with lime wedges, salsa, or hot sauce on the side.

Enjoy these creative Ramen Tacos as a fun and flavorful twist on traditional tacos, combining the crunch of ramen noodles with the savory goodness of taco fillings!

Ramen Casserole

Ingredients:

- 2 packs of instant ramen noodles (discard seasoning packets)
- 1 pound ground beef or chicken (you can also use cooked shredded chicken or tofu)
- 1 small onion, finely chopped
- 1 bell pepper, diced
- 1 cup frozen peas and carrots (or mixed vegetables of your choice)
- 1 can (10.5 oz) condensed cream of mushroom soup (or cream of chicken soup)
- 1 cup milk
- 1 cup shredded cheddar cheese
- Salt and pepper to taste
- Optional toppings: chopped parsley, breadcrumbs, additional cheese for topping

Instructions:

1. **Prepare Ramen Noodles:**
    - Cook the instant ramen noodles according to package instructions, but slightly undercook them to keep them firm. Drain and set aside.
2. **Cook Ground Meat (or Prepare Protein):**
    - In a large skillet, cook ground beef or chicken over medium-high heat until browned and cooked through. Drain excess fat if necessary.
    - If using cooked shredded chicken or tofu, skip this step and proceed to the next.
3. **Sauté Vegetables:**
    - Add chopped onion and diced bell pepper to the skillet with the cooked meat. Cook for 3-4 minutes until vegetables are softened.
    - Stir in frozen peas and carrots (or mixed vegetables). Cook for another 2-3 minutes until heated through. Remove from heat.
4. **Prepare Sauce:**
    - In a mixing bowl, combine condensed cream of mushroom (or cream of chicken) soup and milk. Mix well until smooth.
5. **Assemble Ramen Casserole:**
    - Preheat your oven to 350°F (175°C).
    - In a large mixing bowl, combine the cooked ramen noodles, cooked meat and vegetable mixture, and shredded cheddar cheese. Mix until evenly combined.
    - Pour the soup mixture over the noodle mixture. Stir gently to coat everything in the sauce.
    - Season with salt and pepper to taste.
6. **Bake the Casserole:**
    - Transfer the mixture to a greased 9x13-inch baking dish or a casserole dish of similar size.
    - Optional: Sprinkle chopped parsley, breadcrumbs, or additional shredded cheese on top for extra flavor and texture.

- Cover the dish with foil and bake in the preheated oven for 25-30 minutes, or until heated through and bubbly.

7. **Serve:**
   - Remove from the oven and let it rest for a few minutes before serving.
   - Serve the Ramen Casserole hot as a comforting and satisfying meal.

This Ramen Casserole is a versatile dish that can be customized with your favorite ingredients and makes for a delicious family dinner or potluck dish. Enjoy the creamy texture and flavors of this comforting casserole!

Ramen Sliders

Ingredients:

- 2 packs of instant ramen noodles (discard seasoning packets)
- 1 pound ground beef (or ground chicken, turkey, or tofu)
- Salt and pepper to taste
- 1 tablespoon vegetable oil
- Sliced cheese (cheddar, American, or your favorite)
- Slider toppings (lettuce, tomato slices, pickles, etc.)
- Condiments (mayonnaise, ketchup, mustard, etc.)

Instructions:

1. **Prepare Ramen Noodles:**
    - Cook the instant ramen noodles according to package instructions, but slightly undercook them to keep them firm. Drain and rinse the noodles under cold water to stop the cooking process. Let them cool slightly.
2. **Form Ramen Buns:**
    - Divide the cooked ramen noodles into portions suitable for sliders (about palm-sized portions). Press each portion firmly into a round mold or shape them by hand into bun-sized patties (about 3-4 inches in diameter). Ensure the noodles are packed tightly together.
3. **Cook Ramen Buns:**
    - Heat a large non-stick skillet or griddle over medium heat. Brush lightly with vegetable oil.
    - Carefully transfer the formed ramen noodle buns to the skillet. Cook for about 3-4 minutes on each side until lightly golden and crispy. Press down gently with a spatula to flatten them slightly. Remove from heat and set aside.
4. **Cook Slider Patties:**
    - Season the ground beef (or other protein) with salt and pepper. Divide into portions slightly smaller than the ramen buns.
    - In the same skillet or griddle used for the ramen buns, cook the slider patties over medium-high heat for about 2-3 minutes per side, or until cooked to your desired doneness. During the last minute of cooking, place a slice of cheese on each patty to melt.
5. **Assemble Ramen Sliders:**
    - Place a ramen noodle bun on a serving plate.
    - Top with a slider patty with melted cheese.
    - Add slider toppings such as lettuce, tomato slices, pickles, and any other toppings you prefer.
    - Spread condiments such as mayonnaise, ketchup, mustard, etc., on the inside of the top ramen bun.
6. **Serve:**
    - Secure each Ramen Slider with a toothpick if needed.

- Serve immediately while hot, and enjoy the unique and flavorful Ramen Sliders!

This recipe offers a fun and inventive way to enjoy sliders with a twist using ramen noodles as buns. Customize your Ramen Sliders with your favorite toppings and condiments for a delicious and satisfying meal or party snack!

Ramen Sushi Rolls

Ingredients:

- 2 packs of instant ramen noodles (discard seasoning packets)
- 1 cup sushi rice
- 1 1/4 cups water
- 2 tablespoons rice vinegar
- 1 tablespoon sugar
- 1/2 teaspoon salt
- Nori sheets (seaweed sheets)
- Assorted sushi fillings (e.g., avocado slices, cucumber sticks, cooked shrimp, crab sticks, smoked salmon, etc.)
- Soy sauce, for serving
- Wasabi paste, for serving
- Pickled ginger, for serving

Instructions:

1. **Cook Ramen Noodles:**
   - Cook the instant ramen noodles according to package instructions, but slightly undercook them to keep them firm. Drain and rinse the noodles under cold water to stop the cooking process. Let them cool slightly.
2. **Prepare Sushi Rice:**
   - Rinse sushi rice under cold water until the water runs clear.
   - In a rice cooker or a pot, combine the rinsed rice and water. Cook according to your rice cooker's instructions or bring to a boil, then reduce heat to low, cover, and simmer for 15-20 minutes until the rice is tender and the water is absorbed.
   - In a small bowl, mix rice vinegar, sugar, and salt until dissolved. Heat the mixture in the microwave for a few seconds to help dissolve the sugar completely.
   - Transfer the cooked rice to a large bowl or a wooden sushi oke (sushi rice mixing bowl). Pour the vinegar mixture over the rice and gently fold it in using a spatula or wooden spoon. Be careful not to smash the rice grains. Let the rice cool to room temperature.
3. **Prepare Ramen Sushi Rolls:**
   - Lay a sheet of nori (seaweed) on a bamboo sushi mat or a clean kitchen towel.
   - Spread a thin layer of sushi rice evenly over the nori sheet, leaving about 1 inch of the nori sheet uncovered at the top.
   - Arrange your chosen sushi fillings (avocado slices, cucumber sticks, cooked shrimp, crab sticks, smoked salmon, etc.) horizontally across the center of the rice.
4. **Roll Ramen Sushi Rolls:**
   - Using the bamboo sushi mat or kitchen towel, carefully roll the nori sheet and rice over the fillings, starting from the bottom edge closest to you.
   - Apply gentle pressure to shape the roll, making sure it's tightly rolled.

- Moisten the uncovered edge of the nori sheet with a little water to seal the roll.
5. **Slice and Serve:**
    - Use a sharp knife to slice the rolled sushi into bite-sized pieces, about 1 inch thick.
    - Arrange the Ramen Sushi Rolls on a serving plate.
    - Serve with soy sauce, wasabi paste, and pickled ginger on the side for dipping.
6. **Enjoy:**
    - Enjoy your homemade Ramen Sushi Rolls as a unique and delicious fusion dish!

This recipe allows for creativity in choosing your sushi fillings and provides a fun way to enjoy the flavors of sushi with the addition of ramen noodles. It's perfect for a sushi night at home or as a delightful appetizer for parties!

Ramen Macaroni and Cheese

Ingredients:

- 2 packs of instant ramen noodles (discard seasoning packets)
- 2 cups elbow macaroni (or any pasta of your choice)
- 2 tablespoons butter
- 2 tablespoons all-purpose flour
- 2 cups milk (whole milk or 2% recommended)
- 2 cups shredded cheddar cheese (or a mix of your favorite cheeses)
- Salt and pepper to taste
- Optional: breadcrumbs for topping, chopped parsley for garnish

Instructions:

1. **Cook Ramen Noodles and Macaroni:**
    - Cook the instant ramen noodles and elbow macaroni separately according to package instructions. Drain and set aside.
2. **Make Cheese Sauce:**
    - In a large saucepan or skillet, melt butter over medium heat.
    - Stir in flour and cook for about 1 minute until smooth and bubbly, stirring constantly.
    - Gradually whisk in milk, stirring constantly to avoid lumps. Cook and stir until mixture thickens and comes to a boil.
3. **Add Cheese:**
    - Reduce heat to low. Gradually stir in shredded cheese until melted and smooth. Season with salt and pepper to taste.
4. **Combine Noodles and Sauce:**
    - Add the cooked ramen noodles and elbow macaroni to the cheese sauce. Stir gently until well combined and evenly coated with the cheese sauce.
5. **Serve:**
    - Optional: Transfer the Ramen Macaroni and Cheese to a baking dish. Sprinkle breadcrumbs over the top for a crispy topping.
    - Garnish with chopped parsley if desired.
    - Serve hot and enjoy the creamy and comforting Ramen Macaroni and Cheese!

This recipe offers a delightful twist on classic mac and cheese by incorporating ramen noodles, providing a unique texture and flavor experience. It's a perfect dish for a quick and satisfying meal that the whole family will enjoy!

Ramen Risotto

Ingredients:

- 2 packs of instant ramen noodles (discard seasoning packets)
- 1 cup Arborio rice (or other risotto rice)
- 4 cups chicken or vegetable broth (homemade or low-sodium)
- 1 tablespoon olive oil
- 1 small onion, finely chopped
- 2 cloves garlic, minced
- 1/2 cup dry white wine (optional)
- 1/2 cup grated Parmesan cheese
- Salt and pepper to taste
- Chopped fresh parsley or chives for garnish (optional)

Instructions:

1. **Prepare Ramen Noodles:**
   - Cook the instant ramen noodles according to package instructions, but slightly undercook them to keep them firm. Drain and set aside.
2. **Prepare Risotto:**
   - In a large saucepan or deep skillet, heat olive oil over medium heat.
   - Add chopped onion and sauté for 3-4 minutes until softened.
   - Stir in minced garlic and cook for another minute until fragrant.
3. **Cook Arborio Rice:**
   - Add Arborio rice to the saucepan with the onions and garlic. Stir to coat the rice with the oil and cook for 1-2 minutes until lightly toasted.
4. **Deglaze with Wine (optional):**
   - Pour in the white wine (if using) and stir continuously until the wine is absorbed by the rice.
5. **Add Broth:**
   - Gradually add the chicken or vegetable broth, one cup at a time, stirring frequently. Allow each addition of broth to be absorbed by the rice before adding the next. This process will take about 20-25 minutes until the rice is creamy and tender.
6. **Incorporate Ramen Noodles:**
   - Once the rice is cooked to a creamy consistency (al dente), stir in the cooked ramen noodles. Mix gently to combine with the risotto.
7. **Add Parmesan Cheese and Season:**
   - Stir in grated Parmesan cheese until melted and incorporated into the risotto.
   - Season with salt and pepper to taste.
8. **Serve:**
   - Remove from heat and let the Ramen Risotto rest for a few minutes.
   - Garnish with chopped fresh parsley or chives if desired.

- - Serve hot, and enjoy the creamy and flavorful Ramen Risotto as a unique twist on traditional risotto!

This recipe combines the best of both worlds, blending the creamy texture of risotto with the comforting appeal of ramen noodles. It's a dish that's sure to impress and satisfy!

Ramen Stuffed Peppers

Ingredients:

- 4 bell peppers (any color), tops cut off and seeds removed
- 2 packs of instant ramen noodles (discard seasoning packets)
- 1 pound ground beef (or ground turkey, chicken, or tofu for vegetarian option)
- 1 small onion, finely chopped
- 2 cloves garlic, minced
- 1 cup diced tomatoes (canned or fresh)
- 1 cup shredded cheese (cheddar, mozzarella, or your favorite)
- Salt and pepper to taste
- Optional: chopped fresh herbs (such as parsley or basil) for garnish

Instructions:

1. **Prepare Bell Peppers:**
    - Preheat your oven to 375°F (190°C).
    - Cut the tops off the bell peppers and remove the seeds and membranes. Set aside.
2. **Cook Ramen Noodles:**
    - Cook the instant ramen noodles according to package instructions, but slightly undercook them to keep them firm. Drain and set aside.
3. **Prepare Filling:**
    - In a large skillet, cook the ground beef (or your choice of protein) over medium-high heat until browned and cooked through. Drain excess fat if necessary.
    - Add chopped onion and minced garlic to the skillet with the cooked meat. Cook for 3-4 minutes until onions are softened.
4. **Combine Filling Ingredients:**
    - Stir in diced tomatoes and cooked ramen noodles into the skillet with the meat mixture. Mix well to combine.
    - Season with salt and pepper to taste. Remove from heat.
5. **Stuff Peppers:**
    - Place the hollowed-out bell peppers upright in a baking dish or casserole dish.
    - Spoon the ramen and meat mixture evenly into each bell pepper until they are filled to the top.
6. **Bake:**
    - Cover the baking dish with foil and bake in the preheated oven for 30-35 minutes, or until the peppers are tender.
7. **Add Cheese and Finish:**
    - Remove the foil from the baking dish. Sprinkle shredded cheese evenly over each stuffed pepper.
    - Return the dish to the oven and bake, uncovered, for an additional 5-10 minutes, or until the cheese is melted and bubbly.

8. **Serve:**
    - Remove from the oven and let the Ramen Stuffed Peppers cool slightly before serving.
    - Garnish with chopped fresh herbs if desired.
    - Serve hot and enjoy the unique and flavorful Ramen Stuffed Peppers!

This recipe offers a delicious and creative way to enjoy stuffed peppers with the added twist of ramen noodles, making it a satisfying meal that's sure to be a hit at the dinner table!

Ramen Stew

Ingredients:

- 2 packs of instant ramen noodles (discard seasoning packets)
- 1 pound stew meat (beef, pork, or chicken), cut into bite-sized pieces
- 1 onion, chopped
- 2 cloves garlic, minced
- 2 carrots, sliced
- 2 potatoes, peeled and diced
- 1 cup frozen peas
- 6 cups beef or chicken broth
- 2 tablespoons soy sauce
- 1 tablespoon Worcestershire sauce
- Salt and pepper to taste
- Optional: chopped fresh parsley or green onions for garnish

Instructions:

1. **Brown the Meat:**
    - In a large pot or Dutch oven, heat a bit of oil over medium-high heat.
    - Add the stew meat and cook until browned on all sides. Remove the meat from the pot and set aside.
2. **Sauté Vegetables:**
    - In the same pot, add chopped onion and minced garlic. Sauté for 2-3 minutes until softened and fragrant.
3. **Add Broth and Simmer:**
    - Return the browned meat to the pot.
    - Pour in the beef or chicken broth, soy sauce, and Worcestershire sauce.
    - Bring to a boil, then reduce the heat to low. Cover and simmer for about 1 hour, or until the meat is tender.
4. **Add Potatoes and Carrots:**
    - Add the diced potatoes and sliced carrots to the pot. Stir to combine.
    - Cover and simmer for another 20-30 minutes, or until the vegetables are tender.
5. **Cook Ramen Noodles:**
    - Meanwhile, cook the instant ramen noodles according to package instructions. Drain and set aside.
6. **Combine and Serve:**
    - Once the vegetables are tender, add the cooked ramen noodles and frozen peas to the pot.
    - Stir gently to combine and heat through.
    - Season with salt and pepper to taste.
7. **Serve:**
    - Ladle the Ramen Stew into bowls.
    - Garnish with chopped fresh parsley or green onions if desired.

- Serve hot and enjoy this hearty and comforting Ramen Stew!

This recipe allows for customization with your favorite vegetables and protein, making it a satisfying and warming meal perfect for cooler days or whenever you crave a hearty stew with a twist of ramen noodles.

Ramen Gyoza

Ingredients:

- 2 packs of instant ramen noodles (discard seasoning packets)
- 1/2 pound ground pork (or chicken, turkey, or tofu for vegetarian option)
- 1 cup shredded cabbage
- 2-3 green onions, finely chopped
- 2 cloves garlic, minced
- 1 tablespoon soy sauce
- 1 tablespoon sesame oil
- 1 teaspoon grated ginger
- Salt and pepper, to taste
- 1 tablespoon cornstarch
- 1/4 cup water
- Gyoza wrappers (round or square)
- Vegetable oil, for frying
- Soy sauce, for dipping

Instructions:

1. **Cook Ramen Noodles:**
    - Cook the instant ramen noodles according to package instructions, but slightly undercook them to keep them firm. Drain, rinse with cold water, and set aside to cool.
2. **Prepare Filling:**
    - In a large bowl, combine the cooked ramen noodles (cut into smaller pieces), ground pork (or alternative), shredded cabbage, chopped green onions, minced garlic, soy sauce, sesame oil, grated ginger, salt, and pepper. Mix well until thoroughly combined.
3. **Assemble Gyoza:**
    - In a small bowl, mix cornstarch and water to create a slurry.
    - Take a gyoza wrapper and place a spoonful of the ramen filling in the center (about 1 tablespoon).
    - Dip your finger in the cornstarch slurry and run it along the edge of the wrapper.
    - Fold the wrapper in half over the filling, pressing the edges together to seal. You can pleat the edges for a decorative touch, if desired. Repeat until all filling is used.
4. **Cook Gyoza:**
    - Heat a large non-stick skillet or frying pan over medium-high heat. Add enough vegetable oil to coat the bottom of the pan.
    - Place the gyoza in the pan, flat side down, making sure they are not touching each other.
    - Cook for 2-3 minutes, or until the bottoms are golden brown.
    - Carefully add about 1/4 cup of water to the pan (it will sizzle and steam).

- Immediately cover the pan with a lid and reduce the heat to medium-low. Steam the gyoza for about 5-6 minutes, or until the water has evaporated and the filling is cooked through.
5. **Serve:**
    - Remove the lid from the pan and let the gyoza cook for another minute to crisp up the bottoms.
    - Transfer the Ramen Gyoza to a serving plate.
    - Serve hot with soy sauce for dipping.
6. **Enjoy:**
    - Enjoy your homemade Ramen Gyoza as a delicious appetizer or main dish with a unique twist of ramen noodles!

This recipe offers a fun and flavorful way to enjoy gyoza with the addition of ramen noodles, combining crunchy textures with savory fillings for a delightful Japanese-inspired treat.

Ramen Spring Rolls

Ingredients:

- 2 packs of instant ramen noodles (discard seasoning packets)
- Rice paper wrappers (large size)
- Assorted vegetables and herbs (such as lettuce, cucumber, carrot, bell pepper, avocado, mint, cilantro, etc.)
- Cooked protein of your choice (shrimp, chicken, tofu, etc.) - optional
- Soy sauce or hoisin sauce, for dipping

Instructions:

1. **Prepare Ramen Noodles:**
    - Cook the instant ramen noodles according to package instructions. Drain, rinse with cold water, and set aside to cool.
2. **Prepare Vegetables and Herbs:**
    - Wash and prepare your vegetables and herbs. Cut them into thin strips or julienne.
    - If using protein, ensure it is cooked and cut into strips or small pieces.
3. **Prepare Rice Paper Wrappers:**
    - Fill a shallow dish or large bowl with warm water.
    - Dip one rice paper wrapper into the water and rotate it for a few seconds until it softens and becomes pliable.
    - Lay the softened wrapper flat on a clean surface, such as a cutting board or a damp kitchen towel.
4. **Assemble Ramen Spring Rolls:**
    - Place a small handful of cooked ramen noodles in the center of the rice paper wrapper.
    - Add a few strips of vegetables and herbs on top of the noodles.
    - If using, add a few pieces of cooked protein.
    - Fold the bottom edge of the wrapper over the filling.
    - Fold in the sides of the wrapper, then continue rolling up tightly to form a spring roll.
5. **Repeat:**
    - Continue assembling the Ramen Spring Rolls with the remaining ingredients.
6. **Serve:**
    - Serve the Ramen Spring Rolls whole, or cut them in half diagonally for a decorative presentation.
    - Serve with soy sauce or hoisin sauce for dipping.
7. **Enjoy:**
    - Enjoy your homemade Ramen Spring Rolls as a refreshing and healthy appetizer or light meal, combining the crunch of vegetables with the unique texture of ramen noodles!

These Ramen Spring Rolls are customizable based on your preferences, making them perfect for a quick and delicious snack or a colorful addition to any meal.

Ramen Quiche

Ingredients:

- 2 packs of instant ramen noodles (discard seasoning packets)
- 1 cup shredded cheese (cheddar, mozzarella, or your favorite)
- 4 large eggs
- 1 cup milk or half-and-half
- 1/2 cup diced ham or cooked bacon (optional)
- 1/2 cup diced vegetables (such as bell peppers, spinach, onions, etc.)
- Salt and pepper to taste
- Cooking spray or butter, for greasing the quiche pan
- Optional: chopped fresh herbs for garnish (such as parsley or chives)

Instructions:

1. **Prepare Ramen Noodles:**
   - Cook the instant ramen noodles according to package instructions. Drain and rinse with cold water to cool them down. Set aside.
2. **Preheat Oven:**
   - Preheat your oven to 350°F (175°C). Grease a 9-inch pie dish or quiche pan with cooking spray or butter.
3. **Prepare Quiche Filling:**
   - In a large mixing bowl, whisk together eggs and milk (or half-and-half) until well combined.
   - Stir in cooked ramen noodles, shredded cheese, diced ham or bacon (if using), diced vegetables, salt, and pepper. Mix until evenly distributed.
4. **Assemble and Bake:**
   - Pour the quiche mixture into the prepared pie dish or quiche pan.
   - Smooth out the top with a spatula to ensure even distribution of ingredients.
5. **Bake Quiche:**
   - Bake in the preheated oven for 30-35 minutes, or until the quiche is set and the top is golden brown.
6. **Cool and Serve:**
   - Remove the Ramen Quiche from the oven and let it cool for a few minutes before slicing.
   - Garnish with chopped fresh herbs if desired.
   - Serve warm or at room temperature, and enjoy this unique and flavorful Ramen Quiche!

This recipe allows for versatility by adding your favorite ingredients to the quiche filling. It's a delicious way to enjoy ramen noodles in a new and unexpected dish that's perfect for brunch, lunch, or a light dinner!

Ramen Frittata

Ingredients:

- 2 packs of instant ramen noodles (discard seasoning packets)
- 6 large eggs
- 1/2 cup milk or half-and-half
- 1 cup shredded cheese (cheddar, mozzarella, or your favorite)
- 1 cup diced vegetables (such as bell peppers, spinach, onions, mushrooms, etc.)
- 1/2 cup diced cooked ham, bacon, or cooked sausage (optional)
- Salt and pepper, to taste
- Cooking spray or butter, for greasing the skillet

Instructions:

1. **Prepare Ramen Noodles:**
   - Cook the instant ramen noodles according to package instructions. Drain and rinse with cold water to cool them down. Set aside.
2. **Preheat Oven:**
   - Preheat your oven to 350°F (175°C).
3. **Prepare Frittata Mixture:**
   - In a large mixing bowl, whisk together eggs and milk (or half-and-half) until well combined.
   - Stir in cooked ramen noodles, shredded cheese, diced vegetables, diced cooked ham or other protein (if using), salt, and pepper. Mix until evenly distributed.
4. **Cook Frittata:**
   - Heat a 10-inch oven-safe skillet over medium heat. Coat the skillet with cooking spray or melt a bit of butter.
   - Pour the frittata mixture into the skillet, spreading it evenly with a spatula.
   - Cook on the stovetop for 4-5 minutes, or until the edges begin to set.
5. **Finish in the Oven:**
   - Transfer the skillet to the preheated oven.
   - Bake for 15-20 minutes, or until the frittata is set in the center and lightly golden on top.
6. **Cool and Serve:**
   - Remove the Ramen Frittata from the oven and let it cool for a few minutes before slicing.
   - Slice into wedges and serve warm.
7. **Enjoy:**
   - Enjoy your Ramen Frittata as a hearty and satisfying meal, perfect for breakfast, brunch, or a quick dinner!

This recipe allows for flexibility by incorporating your favorite vegetables and protein into the frittata. It's a creative way to enjoy the flavors and textures of ramen noodles in a comforting and versatile dish.

Ramen Omelette

Ingredients:

- 2 packs of instant ramen noodles (discard seasoning packets)
- 4 large eggs
- 1/2 cup shredded cheese (cheddar, mozzarella, or your favorite)
- 1/2 cup diced vegetables (such as bell peppers, spinach, onions, mushrooms, etc.)
- 1/2 cup diced cooked ham, bacon, or cooked sausage (optional)
- Salt and pepper, to taste
- Cooking spray or butter, for greasing the skillet

Instructions:

1. **Prepare Ramen Noodles:**
    - Cook the instant ramen noodles according to package instructions. Drain and rinse with cold water to cool them down. Set aside.
2. **Prepare Omelette Mixture:**
    - In a large mixing bowl, whisk together eggs until well beaten.
    - Stir in cooked ramen noodles, shredded cheese, diced vegetables, diced cooked ham or other protein (if using), salt, and pepper. Mix until evenly combined.
3. **Cook Omelette:**
    - Heat a non-stick skillet (preferably 10 inches in diameter) over medium heat. Coat the skillet with cooking spray or melt a bit of butter.
    - Pour the egg and ramen mixture into the skillet, spreading it evenly with a spatula.
4. **Cook Until Set:**
    - Cook the omelette for 3-4 minutes, or until the edges start to set and the bottom is golden brown.
5. **Flip or Fold:**
    - Carefully flip one half of the omelette over the other with a spatula to create a half-moon shape. Alternatively, fold the omelette in half directly in the skillet.
6. **Finish Cooking:**
    - Continue cooking for another 2-3 minutes, or until the omelette is completely set and the cheese is melted.
7. **Serve:**
    - Slide the Ramen Omelette onto a serving plate.
    - Cut into slices and serve warm.
8. **Enjoy:**
    - Enjoy your Ramen Omelette as a delicious and filling meal, perfect for breakfast, brunch, or a quick dinner!

This recipe is customizable, allowing you to add your favorite vegetables, meats, or cheeses to suit your taste preferences. It's a fun and creative way to incorporate ramen noodles into a classic omelette dish.

Ramen Breakfast Bowl

Ingredients:

- 2 packs of instant ramen noodles (discard seasoning packets)
- 4 large eggs
- 1 cup diced vegetables (such as bell peppers, spinach, onions, mushrooms, etc.)
- 1/2 cup diced cooked ham, bacon, or cooked sausage (optional)
- 1/2 avocado, sliced
- Soy sauce or tamari, to taste
- Sriracha or hot sauce, to taste (optional)
- Sesame seeds, for garnish
- Chopped green onions, for garnish
- Salt and pepper, to taste

Instructions:

1. **Prepare Ramen Noodles:**
    - Cook the instant ramen noodles according to package instructions. Drain and set aside.
2. **Cook Eggs:**
    - In a non-stick skillet, cook the eggs to your preference (fried, scrambled, or poached).
3. **Prepare Vegetables and Protein:**
    - In the same skillet or another, sauté the diced vegetables until tender. Add the diced ham, bacon, or sausage (if using) and cook until heated through.
4. **Assemble Breakfast Bowl:**
    - Divide the cooked ramen noodles among serving bowls.
    - Top with the cooked vegetables and protein mixture.
5. **Add Eggs and Avocado:**
    - Place the cooked eggs on top of the noodles and vegetables.
    - Add sliced avocado to the bowl.
6. **Season and Garnish:**
    - Drizzle soy sauce or tamari over the bowl to taste.
    - Add sriracha or hot sauce if desired for extra spice.
    - Sprinkle sesame seeds and chopped green onions over the bowl.
    - Season with salt and pepper to taste.
7. **Serve:**
    - Serve the Ramen Breakfast Bowl immediately while warm.
8. **Enjoy:**
    - Enjoy your Ramen Breakfast Bowl as a hearty and flavorful start to your day, combining the comfort of ramen noodles with the nutrition of eggs, vegetables, and avocado!

This recipe can be easily customized with your favorite breakfast ingredients and seasonings, making it a versatile and satisfying morning meal.

Ramen Hash Browns

Ingredients:

- 2 packs of instant ramen noodles (discard seasoning packets)
- 2 cups shredded potatoes (about 2 medium potatoes)
- 1/4 cup finely chopped onion
- 1/4 cup all-purpose flour
- 2 large eggs, beaten
- Salt and pepper, to taste
- Cooking oil (vegetable or canola), for frying

Instructions:

1. **Prepare Ramen Noodles:**
   - Cook the instant ramen noodles according to package instructions. Drain and rinse with cold water to cool them down. Set aside.
2. **Prepare Potatoes:**
   - Peel and grate the potatoes using a box grater or a food processor. Place the grated potatoes in a clean kitchen towel and squeeze out excess moisture.
3. **Combine Ingredients:**
   - In a large mixing bowl, combine the cooked ramen noodles, shredded potatoes, finely chopped onion, flour, beaten eggs, salt, and pepper. Mix well until all ingredients are evenly distributed.
4. **Form Hash Browns:**
   - Heat a large non-stick skillet or griddle over medium heat. Add enough cooking oil to coat the bottom of the skillet.
   - Take a portion of the ramen-potato mixture (about 1/4 cup) and form it into a patty or round shape with your hands. Place it in the skillet and flatten it slightly with a spatula.
5. **Cook Hash Browns:**
   - Cook the hash browns for 3-4 minutes on each side, or until golden brown and crispy. Flip carefully to avoid breaking them.
6. **Repeat:**
   - Cook the remaining ramen-potato mixture in batches, adding more oil to the skillet as needed.
7. **Serve:**
   - Transfer the cooked Ramen Hash Browns to a plate lined with paper towels to drain excess oil.
   - Serve hot as a delicious and unique side dish or breakfast item.
8. **Enjoy:**
   - Enjoy your Ramen Hash Browns on their own or with your favorite toppings or sauces!

This recipe offers a fun twist on traditional hash browns by incorporating ramen noodles, adding a delightful crunch and texture to a classic dish.

Ramen Pancakes

Ingredients:

- 2 packs of instant ramen noodles (discard seasoning packets)
- 1 cup all-purpose flour
- 1 cup milk
- 2 large eggs
- 2 tablespoons sugar
- 1 teaspoon baking powder
- 1/2 teaspoon salt
- Cooking oil or butter, for cooking

Instructions:

1. **Prepare Ramen Noodles:**
   - Cook the instant ramen noodles according to package instructions. Drain and rinse with cold water to cool them down. Set aside.
2. **Prepare Pancake Batter:**
   - In a large mixing bowl, combine the cooked ramen noodles (make sure they are well-drained and cooled), all-purpose flour, milk, eggs, sugar, baking powder, and salt. Mix well until smooth and evenly combined.
3. **Cook Pancakes:**
   - Heat a non-stick skillet or griddle over medium heat. Lightly grease the skillet with cooking oil or butter.
   - Pour about 1/4 cup of the pancake batter onto the skillet for each pancake. Spread it slightly with a spoon or ladle to form a round shape.
4. **Cook Until Golden Brown:**
   - Cook the pancakes for 2-3 minutes, or until bubbles form on the surface and the edges look set.
   - Flip the pancakes and cook for another 1-2 minutes, or until golden brown and cooked through.
5. **Repeat:**
   - Repeat with the remaining batter, adding more oil or butter to the skillet as needed.
6. **Serve:**
   - Serve the Ramen Pancakes warm, topped with butter, maple syrup, honey, or your favorite pancake toppings.
7. **Enjoy:**
   - Enjoy your Ramen Pancakes as a creative and flavorful breakfast or brunch option!

These Ramen Pancakes offer a playful twist on traditional pancakes, adding a unique texture and subtle flavor from the ramen noodles. They are sure to be a hit with both kids and adults alike!

Ramen Donuts

Ingredients:

- 2 packs of instant ramen noodles (discard seasoning packets)
- 1 cup all-purpose flour
- 1/2 cup granulated sugar
- 1 teaspoon baking powder
- 1/4 teaspoon salt
- 2 large eggs
- 1/2 cup milk
- 1 teaspoon vanilla extract
- Oil for frying (vegetable or canola)

Optional Glaze:

- 1 cup powdered sugar
- 2-3 tablespoons milk or water
- 1/2 teaspoon vanilla extract

Instructions:

1. **Prepare Ramen Noodles:**
    - Cook the instant ramen noodles according to package instructions. Drain and rinse with cold water to cool them down. Set aside.
2. **Prepare Donut Batter:**
    - In a large mixing bowl, combine the cooked ramen noodles (make sure they are well-drained and cooled), all-purpose flour, granulated sugar, baking powder, and salt.
3. **Mix Wet Ingredients:**
    - In another bowl, whisk together the eggs, milk, and vanilla extract.
4. **Combine Wet and Dry Ingredients:**
    - Pour the wet ingredients into the dry ingredients (including the ramen noodles). Stir until just combined. Do not overmix.
5. **Heat Oil:**
    - Heat oil in a deep fryer or heavy-bottomed pot to 350°F (175°C).
6. **Form and Fry Donuts:**
    - Drop spoonfuls of the batter into the hot oil using a spoon or a cookie scoop. You can shape them slightly with wet hands if needed, or use a piping bag for more precise shapes.
    - Fry the donuts for about 2-3 minutes per side, or until golden brown and cooked through. Fry in batches, making sure not to overcrowd the pot.
7. **Drain and Cool:**
    - Remove the donuts from the oil using a slotted spoon and place them on a plate lined with paper towels to drain excess oil. Let them cool slightly.

8. **Optional Glaze:**
    - In a small bowl, whisk together powdered sugar, milk or water, and vanilla extract until smooth.
    - Dip each cooled donut into the glaze, allowing excess glaze to drip off. Place them on a wire rack set over a baking sheet to catch drips.
9. **Serve:**
    - Allow the glaze to set for a few minutes before serving the Ramen Donuts.
10. **Enjoy:**
    - Enjoy your unique and delicious Ramen Donuts as a fun and unexpected treat!

These Ramen Donuts offer a playful twist on traditional donuts, incorporating ramen noodles for a delightful texture. They make for a memorable dessert or snack that's sure to surprise and delight!

Ramen Ice Cream

Ingredients:

- 2 packs of instant ramen noodles (discard seasoning packets)
- 2 cups whole milk
- 1 cup heavy cream
- 3/4 cup granulated sugar
- 4 large egg yolks
- 1 teaspoon vanilla extract
- Pinch of salt

Optional Toppings:

- Crushed peanuts or almonds
- Caramel sauce
- Honey or maple syrup

Instructions:

1. **Prepare Ramen Noodles:**
    - Cook the instant ramen noodles according to package instructions. Drain and rinse with cold water to cool them down. Set aside.
2. **Make Ramen Infused Milk:**
    - In a saucepan, heat the milk and heavy cream over medium heat until it begins to simmer. Stir occasionally to prevent scorching.
    - Once simmering, add the cooked ramen noodles to the milk mixture. Let it steep for about 15-20 minutes, stirring occasionally to infuse the flavors.
3. **Strain the Mixture:**
    - After steeping, strain the milk mixture through a fine-mesh sieve or cheesecloth to remove the ramen noodles. Press down gently on the noodles to extract maximum flavor.
4. **Prepare the Ice Cream Base:**
    - In a separate bowl, whisk together the egg yolks and sugar until pale and creamy.
5. **Temper the Eggs:**
    - Gradually pour the warm milk mixture into the egg yolk mixture, whisking constantly to temper the eggs. This prevents them from scrambling.
6. **Cook the Custard:**
    - Transfer the mixture back to the saucepan and cook over medium-low heat, stirring constantly with a wooden spoon, until the custard thickens enough to coat the back of the spoon. Do not let it boil.
7. **Cool the Custard:**
    - Remove the custard from the heat and stir in the vanilla extract and a pinch of salt. Allow the mixture to cool to room temperature.

8. **Chill the Custard:**
    - Cover the custard with plastic wrap, pressing it directly onto the surface to prevent a skin from forming. Chill in the refrigerator for at least 4 hours or overnight until thoroughly chilled.
9. **Churn the Ice Cream:**
    - Pour the chilled custard into an ice cream maker and churn according to the manufacturer's instructions until it reaches a soft-serve consistency.
10. **Freeze the Ice Cream:**
    - Transfer the churned ice cream into a freezer-safe container. If desired, swirl in any optional toppings like crushed peanuts, almonds, caramel sauce, or honey.
    - Freeze the ice cream for at least 4 hours or until firm.
11. **Serve:**
    - Scoop the Ramen Ice Cream into bowls or cones.
    - Garnish with additional toppings if desired.
    - Enjoy your unique and flavorful Ramen Ice Cream creation!

This recipe offers a playful and unexpected twist on traditional ice cream, infusing it with the savory notes of ramen noodles. It's sure to be a conversation starter at any gathering!

Ramen Pudding

Ingredients:

- 2 packs of instant ramen noodles (discard seasoning packets)
- 4 cups whole milk
- 1/2 cup granulated sugar
- 4 large eggs
- 1 teaspoon vanilla extract
- Pinch of salt
- Optional toppings: crushed nuts, whipped cream, fresh fruit

Instructions:

1. **Prepare Ramen Noodles:**
    - Cook the instant ramen noodles according to package instructions. Drain and rinse with cold water to cool them down. Set aside.
2. **Make Ramen Infused Milk:**
    - In a saucepan, heat the milk over medium heat until it begins to simmer. Stir occasionally to prevent scorching.
    - Once simmering, add the cooked ramen noodles to the milk. Let it steep for about 15-20 minutes, stirring occasionally to infuse the flavors.
3. **Strain the Mixture:**
    - After steeping, strain the milk mixture through a fine-mesh sieve or cheesecloth to remove the ramen noodles. Press down gently on the noodles to extract maximum flavor.
4. **Prepare the Pudding Base:**
    - In a large mixing bowl, whisk together sugar, eggs, vanilla extract, and a pinch of salt until well combined.
5. **Temper the Eggs:**
    - Gradually pour the warm milk mixture into the egg mixture, whisking constantly to temper the eggs. This prevents them from scrambling.
6. **Cook the Pudding:**
    - Transfer the mixture back to the saucepan and cook over medium-low heat, stirring constantly with a wooden spoon, until the pudding thickens enough to coat the back of the spoon. Do not let it boil.
7. **Cool the Pudding:**
    - Remove the pudding from the heat and pour it into serving dishes or ramekins.
    - Let the pudding cool to room temperature, then refrigerate for at least 2 hours or until chilled and set.
8. **Serve:**
    - Serve the Ramen Pudding chilled, optionally topped with crushed nuts, whipped cream, or fresh fruit.
9. **Enjoy:**

- Enjoy your unique and delicious Ramen Pudding as a creative dessert that combines the comfort of pudding with the unexpected twist of ramen noodles!

This recipe offers a fun and flavorful way to enjoy pudding, infusing it with the savory essence of ramen noodles for a delightful and memorable dessert experience.

Ramen Cheesecake

Ingredients:

For the Crust:

- 1 pack of instant ramen noodles (discard seasoning packet)
- 1/4 cup unsalted butter, melted
- 1/4 cup granulated sugar

For the Cheesecake Filling:

- 16 oz (450g) cream cheese, softened
- 1/2 cup granulated sugar
- 2 large eggs
- 1/2 cup sour cream
- 1 teaspoon vanilla extract
- Zest of 1 lemon (optional)

Optional Toppings:

- Whipped cream
- Fresh berries or fruit compote

Instructions:

1. **Prepare Ramen Crust:**
    - Preheat your oven to 350°F (175°C). Grease a 9-inch springform pan with butter or cooking spray.
    - Cook the instant ramen noodles according to package instructions. Drain and discard any seasoning packets.
    - In a food processor, pulse the cooked ramen noodles until they resemble coarse crumbs.
    - In a bowl, mix together the ramen crumbs, melted butter, and granulated sugar until well combined.
    - Press the mixture firmly into the bottom of the prepared springform pan to form an even crust.
2. **Prepare Cheesecake Filling:**
    - In a large mixing bowl, beat the softened cream cheese and granulated sugar with an electric mixer until smooth and creamy.
    - Add the eggs one at a time, mixing well after each addition.
    - Mix in the sour cream, vanilla extract, and lemon zest (if using), until smooth and well combined.
3. **Assemble and Bake:**
    - Pour the cheesecake filling over the prepared ramen crust in the springform pan.
    - Smooth the top with a spatula to ensure an even layer.

4. **Bake Cheesecake:**
   - Place the springform pan on a baking sheet (to catch any potential drips) and bake in the preheated oven for 45-50 minutes, or until the edges are set and the center is slightly jiggly.
5. **Cool and Chill:**
   - Turn off the oven and leave the cheesecake inside with the door slightly ajar for about 1 hour to cool gradually.
   - Remove the cheesecake from the oven and let it cool completely at room temperature.
   - Once cooled, refrigerate the cheesecake for at least 4 hours or overnight to set completely.
6. **Serve:**
   - Remove the chilled Ramen Cheesecake from the springform pan and place it on a serving plate.
   - Optionally, garnish with whipped cream and fresh berries or fruit compote.
7. **Enjoy:**
   - Slice and enjoy your unique and delicious Ramen Cheesecake, showcasing the delightful combination of creamy cheesecake with a subtle hint of ramen noodles!

This recipe offers a creative twist on classic cheesecake, incorporating ramen noodles into a dessert that's sure to impress and delight your taste buds!

Ramen Cookies

Ingredients:

- 1 pack of instant ramen noodles (discard seasoning packet)
- 1 cup all-purpose flour
- 1/2 teaspoon baking powder
- 1/4 teaspoon baking soda
- 1/4 teaspoon salt
- 1/2 cup unsalted butter, softened
- 1/2 cup granulated sugar
- 1/4 cup brown sugar
- 1 large egg
- 1 teaspoon vanilla extract
- 1/2 cup chocolate chips or chopped chocolate
- Optional: crushed nuts, coconut flakes, or dried fruit

Instructions:

1. **Prepare Ramen Noodles:**
   - Cook the instant ramen noodles according to package instructions. Drain and rinse with cold water to cool them down. Set aside to cool completely.
2. **Prepare Cookie Dough:**
   - Preheat your oven to 350°F (175°C). Line a baking sheet with parchment paper.
   - Break the cooled ramen noodles into smaller pieces.
3. **Dry Ingredients:**
   - In a bowl, whisk together the flour, baking powder, baking soda, and salt. Set aside.
4. **Cream Butter and Sugars:**
   - In a separate large mixing bowl, cream together the softened butter, granulated sugar, and brown sugar until light and fluffy.
5. **Add Egg and Vanilla:**
   - Beat in the egg and vanilla extract until well combined.
6. **Combine Wet and Dry Ingredients:**
   - Gradually add the flour mixture to the butter-sugar mixture, mixing until just combined.
7. **Fold in Ramen Noodles and Chocolate:**
   - Gently fold in the cooked ramen noodles and chocolate chips (or chopped chocolate) until evenly distributed in the cookie dough. Optionally, add crushed nuts, coconut flakes, or dried fruit.
8. **Form Cookies:**
   - Drop tablespoon-sized balls of dough onto the prepared baking sheet, spacing them about 2 inches apart.
9. **Bake Cookies:**

- Bake in the preheated oven for 10-12 minutes, or until the edges are golden brown.
10. **Cool and Serve:**
    - Remove from the oven and let the cookies cool on the baking sheet for a few minutes before transferring them to a wire rack to cool completely.
11. **Enjoy:**
    - Enjoy your delicious Ramen Cookies as a unique and flavorful treat!

These Ramen Cookies offer a playful twist on traditional cookies, incorporating the crunchy texture of ramen noodles with the sweetness of chocolate chips or other add-ins. They're sure to be a hit with friends and family!

Ramen Granola Bars

Ingredients:

- 2 packs of instant ramen noodles (discard seasoning packets)
- 2 cups rolled oats
- 1/2 cup chopped nuts (such as almonds, pecans, or walnuts)
- 1/2 cup dried fruit (such as raisins, cranberries, or chopped apricots)
- 1/2 cup honey or maple syrup
- 1/4 cup unsalted butter or coconut oil
- 1/4 cup packed brown sugar
- 1 teaspoon vanilla extract
- 1/2 teaspoon salt

Instructions:

1. **Prepare Ramen Noodles:**
    - Cook the instant ramen noodles according to package instructions. Drain and discard any seasoning packets. Let the noodles cool completely, then break them into smaller pieces.
2. **Preheat Oven:**
    - Preheat your oven to 350°F (175°C). Line a 9x13-inch baking dish with parchment paper, leaving some overhang for easy removal later.
3. **Prepare Dry Ingredients:**
    - In a large bowl, combine the cooled ramen noodles, rolled oats, chopped nuts, and dried fruit. Mix well and set aside.
4. **Make Granola Bar Base:**
    - In a small saucepan, combine honey (or maple syrup), butter (or coconut oil), brown sugar, vanilla extract, and salt over medium heat. Stir until the butter melts and the mixture is well combined and smooth.
5. **Combine Wet and Dry Ingredients:**
    - Pour the honey (or maple syrup) mixture over the dry ingredients in the bowl. Stir until all ingredients are evenly coated.
6. **Press into Baking Dish:**
    - Transfer the mixture into the prepared baking dish. Use a spatula or the back of a spoon to press the mixture firmly and evenly into the dish.
7. **Bake:**
    - Bake in the preheated oven for 25-30 minutes, or until the edges are golden brown.
8. **Cool and Slice:**
    - Remove from the oven and let the granola bars cool completely in the baking dish on a wire rack.
9. **Slice into Bars:**
    - Once cooled, lift the granola bars out of the baking dish using the parchment paper overhang. Place on a cutting board and slice into bars of your desired size.

10. **Store:**
    - Store the Ramen Granola Bars in an airtight container at room temperature for up to one week, or in the refrigerator for longer shelf life.
11. **Enjoy:**
    - Enjoy your homemade Ramen Granola Bars as a delicious and crunchy snack on the go or for a quick energy boost!

This recipe allows you to incorporate the unique crunch of ramen noodles into a nutritious and satisfying granola bar, perfect for any time of day.

Ramen Smoothie

Ingredients:

- 1 pack of instant ramen noodles (discard seasoning packet)
- 1 cup milk (dairy or plant-based)
- 1 ripe banana, frozen
- 1/2 cup plain Greek yogurt
- 1 tablespoon honey or maple syrup (optional, adjust sweetness to taste)
- 1/2 teaspoon vanilla extract
- Ice cubes (optional, for desired consistency)

Instructions:

1. **Prepare Ramen Noodles:**
    - Cook the instant ramen noodles according to package instructions. Drain and rinse with cold water to cool them down. Set aside to cool completely.
2. **Blend Ingredients:**
    - In a blender, combine the cooled ramen noodles, milk, frozen banana, Greek yogurt, honey or maple syrup (if using), and vanilla extract.
    - Optionally, add a handful of ice cubes for a colder and thicker smoothie.
3. **Blend Until Smooth:**
    - Blend on high speed until the mixture is smooth and well combined. If the smoothie is too thick, add more milk or a bit of water to adjust the consistency.
4. **Serve:**
    - Pour the Ramen Smoothie into glasses.
    - Optionally, garnish with a sprinkle of cinnamon, nutmeg, or a drizzle of honey on top.
5. **Enjoy:**
    - Enjoy your unique and nutritious Ramen Smoothie as a refreshing and satisfying drink!

This recipe allows you to incorporate the texture of ramen noodles into a smoothie while combining it with the sweetness of banana and the creaminess of Greek yogurt. It's a fun and creative way to enjoy a smoothie with a twist!

Ramen Cocktail

Ingredients:

- 2 packs of instant ramen noodles (discard seasoning packets)
- 2 cups water
- 1 cup vodka or sake
- 1/4 cup soy sauce
- 1 tablespoon sesame oil
- 1 tablespoon rice vinegar
- 1 teaspoon fresh ginger, grated
- Ice cubes
- Optional: garnishes such as sliced green onions, sesame seeds, or a lime wedge

Instructions:

1. **Prepare Ramen Infused Vodka or Sake:**
   - Cook the instant ramen noodles according to package instructions, using only water and discarding the seasoning packets.
   - Drain the cooked ramen noodles and let them cool completely.
   - In a container with a lid, combine the cooled ramen noodles and vodka or sake. Close the lid tightly and let it infuse in the refrigerator for at least 2 hours, shaking occasionally to mix flavors.
2. **Prepare Ramen Cocktail Base:**
   - In a cocktail shaker, combine 1/4 cup of the ramen-infused vodka or sake (strained to remove noodles), soy sauce, sesame oil, rice vinegar, and grated ginger.
   - Fill the cocktail shaker with ice cubes.
3. **Shake and Strain:**
   - Shake the cocktail shaker vigorously for about 15-20 seconds to chill the ingredients well.
4. **Serve:**
   - Strain the cocktail mixture into a chilled cocktail glass.
5. **Garnish and Enjoy:**
   - Garnish the Ramen Cocktail with sliced green onions, sesame seeds, or a lime wedge, if desired.
   - Serve immediately and enjoy the savory and unique flavors of your Ramen Cocktail!

This recipe offers a creative and unexpected twist on traditional cocktails, incorporating the savory notes of ramen noodles infused into vodka or sake, complemented by soy sauce, sesame oil, and ginger. It's sure to be a conversation starter at any gathering! Adjust the ingredients and proportions to suit your taste preferences.

Ramen Infused Water

Ingredients:

- 1 pack of instant ramen noodles (discard seasoning packet)
- 4 cups water
- Optional: Ice cubes, mint leaves, cucumber slices, lemon or lime slices for garnish

Instructions:

1. **Prepare Ramen Noodles:**
    - Cook the instant ramen noodles according to package instructions, using only water and discarding the seasoning packet.
    - Drain the cooked ramen noodles and rinse them briefly with cold water to cool them down.
2. **Infuse the Water:**
    - In a pitcher or large container, combine the cooled ramen noodles with 4 cups of water.
    - Cover the pitcher and refrigerate for at least 1-2 hours to allow the flavors to infuse.
3. **Serve:**
    - Strain the ramen-infused water through a fine-mesh sieve or cheesecloth to remove the noodles.
    - Pour the infused water into glasses filled with ice cubes, if desired.
4. **Garnish and Enjoy:**
    - Optionally, garnish each glass with mint leaves, cucumber slices, or lemon/lime slices for added freshness and flavor.
    - Stir well and enjoy your refreshing Ramen Infused Water!

This Ramen Infused Water provides a subtle and unique twist on traditional infused waters, offering a hint of savory flavor from the ramen noodles. It's a refreshing beverage idea that's perfect for staying hydrated with a touch of creativity!

Ramen Tea

Ingredients:

- 1 pack of instant ramen noodles (discard seasoning packet)
- 2 cups water
- Green tea bag or loose leaf green tea (optional)
- Honey or sweetener, to taste (optional)

Instructions:

1. **Prepare Ramen Noodles:**
    - Cook the instant ramen noodles according to package instructions, using only water and discarding the seasoning packet.
    - Drain the cooked ramen noodles and rinse them briefly with cold water to cool them down.
2. **Infuse the Tea:**
    - In a small saucepan, bring 2 cups of water to a boil.
    - Add the cooled ramen noodles to the boiling water.
    - If desired, add a green tea bag or loose leaf green tea to the saucepan for additional flavor (optional).
3. **Simmer:**
    - Reduce the heat and simmer the mixture for about 5-7 minutes, allowing the flavors to meld together.
4. **Strain and Serve:**
    - Remove the saucepan from heat and strain the liquid through a fine-mesh sieve or cheesecloth to remove the noodles and tea leaves.
5. **Sweeten (Optional) and Enjoy:**
    - Stir in honey or sweetener to taste, if desired.
    - Pour the Ramen Tea into cups and serve it hot.

This Ramen Tea offers a delicate infusion of flavors, combining the comforting essence of ramen noodles with the soothing qualities of green tea. It's a unique and enjoyable beverage option that's perfect for experimenting with different tea blends and flavor combinations.

Ramen Lemonade

Ingredients:

- 1 pack of instant ramen noodles (discard seasoning packet)
- 4 cups water
- 1 cup freshly squeezed lemon juice (about 4-6 lemons)
- 1/2 cup granulated sugar (adjust to taste)
- Ice cubes
- Lemon slices and mint leaves for garnish (optional)

Instructions:

1. **Prepare Ramen Noodles:**
   - Cook the instant ramen noodles according to package instructions, using only water. Drain and rinse the noodles with cold water to cool them down. Set aside.
2. **Make Ramen Infused Water:**
   - In a pitcher, combine 4 cups of water with the cooled ramen noodles. Let it sit for at least 1 hour in the refrigerator to allow the flavors to infuse.
3. **Prepare Lemonade:**
   - In another pitcher, combine freshly squeezed lemon juice and granulated sugar. Stir well until the sugar is dissolved.
4. **Strain and Mix:**
   - Strain the ramen-infused water through a fine-mesh sieve or cheesecloth to remove the noodles. Discard the noodles.
   - Pour the infused water into the pitcher with the lemon juice mixture. Stir well to combine.
5. **Serve:**
   - Fill glasses with ice cubes.
   - Pour the Ramen Lemonade over the ice cubes.
6. **Garnish and Enjoy:**
   - Optionally, garnish each glass with lemon slices and mint leaves for added freshness and presentation.
   - Stir well before drinking and enjoy your refreshing Ramen Lemonade!

This Ramen Lemonade offers a unique twist on traditional lemonade by infusing it with the subtle flavors of ramen noodles. It's a fun and creative beverage idea that's perfect for a hot day or any special occasion! Adjust the sweetness and lemon juice to suit your taste preferences.

Ramen Energy Drink

Ingredients:

- 1 pack of instant ramen noodles (discard seasoning packet)
- 2 cups water
- 1 cup coconut water or sports drink (like Gatorade)
- 1 tablespoon honey or agave syrup
- Juice of 1 lemon or lime
- 1/2 teaspoon grated ginger (optional)
- Pinch of salt
- Ice cubes

Instructions:

1. **Prepare Ramen Noodles:**
   - Cook the instant ramen noodles according to package instructions using only water. Drain and rinse with cold water to cool them down. Set aside.
2. **Make Ramen Infused Base:**
   - In a blender, combine the cooled ramen noodles and 2 cups of water. Blend until the noodles are finely chopped and the mixture is well combined.
3. **Mix Ingredients:**
   - In a large pitcher or container, combine the ramen-infused water with coconut water (or sports drink), honey or agave syrup, lemon or lime juice, grated ginger (if using), and a pinch of salt. Stir well to combine.
4. **Chill:**
   - Refrigerate the mixture for at least 1 hour to allow the flavors to meld together and chill.
5. **Serve:**
   - Fill glasses with ice cubes.
   - Pour the Ramen Energy Drink over the ice cubes.
6. **Enjoy:**
   - Stir well before drinking and enjoy your Ramen Energy Drink as a refreshing and energizing beverage!

This Ramen Energy Drink combines the hydrating properties of coconut water or sports drink with the unique texture of ramen noodles, providing a boost of energy and refreshment. It's a fun and innovative way to enjoy a revitalizing drink! Adjust sweetness and flavorings to suit your preferences.

www.ingramcontent.com/pod-product-compliance
Lightning Source LLC
LaVergne TN
LVHW062047070526
838201LV00080B/2154